MW01028893

THE *HOPE KNOWS* BOOKS:

Getting Through Today

———

Beyond The Past
coming soon

———

Facing Tomorrow
coming soon

———

Can God Be Trusted?
coming soon

HOPE KNOWS

GETTING THROUGH
TODAY

elaine starner

JPV PRESS

Author can be reached at P.O. Box 185, Walnut Creek, OH 44687, or by email at *myhopeknows@gmail.com.*

All other external material referenced has been used by permission.

Printed in the United States of America

First Printing, 2018

ISBN 978-1-946389-05-3

JPV ⚑ PRESS

2106 Main Street / PO Box 201
Winesburg, OH 44690

www.jpvpress.com

This book is dedicated to
every heart set on pilgrimage –
Live with great expectation!

 CONTENTS

The Gift of Hope..1

Everything We Need..17

Promises for Those Who Wait....................................59

Help for Our Hope..77

Carried in His Arms..95

"I'm Here to Help You"..109

Finding New Strength..145

Winning the Battle..165

Rescue From an Empty Life.....................................193

Good Things Out of Hard Places...............................221

Refreshment for the Weary.......................................253

The Great Treasure..271

Walking the Best Path..291

Defense Against Discouragement..............................313

Appendix..331

PRAYER FOR HOPE:

Remember your promise to me;

it is my only hope.

– **PSALM 119:49** –

THE GIFT OF HOPE

IF WE ONLY KNEW...

If you only knew the gift God has for you...
- JOHN 4:10 -

The words above are difficult to shrug off and ignore. Jesus spoke them to a woman He met in His travels.

And He is speaking them to us, today.

They struck my soul at a place that was already aching and stayed embedded there.

Because if I only knew... What then?

If God has something for me, what is it?
And what difference could it make in my life?

Taking a walk during a break in the cold rain one winter day, I thought I saw the flash of a blue wing. A bluebird? Impossible. But sure enough, there it was above me, with cerulean wings and ruddy throat, creating a resplendent banner against the dull, bare branches and gray sky. To my amazement, another sailed overhead and perched on a wire.

Back home, I did a little research and learned that bluebirds winter in our area. I never knew that! I'm just an occasional bird watcher, but I do notice bluebirds; they have a sentimental, symbolic meaning for me, so I love to see them. Yet I had never before noticed or even thought to look for them during the cold seasons. I just didn't know they were there.

Those flashes of blue and rust would be here even on days of cold and snow. I need only watch for them. That happy thought transformed the prospect of a long winter ahead.

"But where are they?" a friend asked when I mentioned my discovery. "Where do they stay? I never see them."

Hope is like my bluebirds. Many people wonder where there is any hope in the world today. They cannot see it. They don't know where to look for it. They may even think it doesn't exist. Their circumstances may seem to blot out any possibility of hope.

Life without hope can seem all too frustrating, frail, fruitless... and dull!

But Almighty God offers us hope. *It is here. In every season.* And it's a gift.

Scriptures say that God has plans for us that are "too numerous to list," and there is much joy waiting for those who trust Him (Psalm 40:4,5).

Can we believe that?

If we only knew...

I wanted to know what hope I can hold onto in this turbulent world. Is there hope? Where do I find it? Does trusting God make any difference in my life?

ᛌᚾᛆᚱ HOPE IS NOT A WISH ᚱᛆᚾᛌ

God has given both his promise and his oath... It is impossible for God to lie... We can have great confidence as we hold to the hope that lies before us.

– HEBREWS 6:18 –

As we begin, let's take a look at what it means when God uses the word *hope.* After all, followers of Jesus Christ have built their lives on this thing called *hope.*

In our conversations today, we use the word hope in so many different ways. It generally means we're *wishing for* something that may or may not be possible. We "hope" we can go. We "hope" someone will come through for us. We "hope" it won't rain during the ball game. We "hope" for success. We've watered down the meaning of this word *hope.*

But in God's vocabulary, *hope* is a certainty that what is promised will happen.

I am grateful to Tyndale House Publishers for giving me a fresh understanding of Christian hope. In their *Holy Bible*, New Living Translation, Second Edition, they include a "Word Study System," that examines the definitions of some of the most frequently used Hebrew and Greek words in the Scriptures. That brief study prompted me to also dig into James Strong's *Exhaustive Concordance.*

And I discovered that hope is much more than a wish.

The Greek word (used in the New Testament) that we have translated into our English word *hope* is *elpis*, and the Hebrew word (in the Old Testament) is *yakhal*. Those two words are words with no doubt or wavering. Both words convey confidence, expectation, and a certainty that something *will* happen.

A Christian's hope is not simply wishful thinking. It's expectation and certainty. It *knows*.

How, then, is hope connected to *faith?*

Here's how I think of hope and faith: *Hope* is the promise of what will be; it's a bridge God has laid before us so that we can confidently move forward as we journey through life. *Faith*, then, is acting on that hope, walking forward over that bridge with certainty that it can be trusted to carry us. God does not lie.

Have you ever started over a bridge and not been able to see the other side or where the road will take you after the bridge? Hope and faith are like that. We go forward, not because we can see exactly where we are going, but because we trust the promise God has given to carry us forward.

We can build our lives on the promises our heavenly Father has made, confidently going forward each day, expecting that He will do what He says He will do.

Imagine that. In today's shifting, ambiguous, and unreliable world, we can still have something solid to depend on!

In God's world, hope is not a wish. It's a bridge we can always trust to carry us forward.

ꞏꞏꞏꞏꞏ WHAT HOPE CAN DO FOR US ꞏꞏꞏꞏꞏ

Blessed are those who trust in the LORD and have made the LORD their hope and confidence. They are like trees planted along a riverbank, with roots that reach deep into the water. Such trees are not bothered by the heat or worried by long months of drought. Their leaves stay green, and they never stop producing fruit.

– JEREMIAH 17:7-8 –

Even those who do not claim to believe in any god know how important hope is to our lives. Listen to daily conversations, and you'll hear this need:

"If only I could see a light at the end of the tunnel..."

"I can't see any hope..."

"As long as there's hope..."

"You can't give up hope..."

The Creator is a God of great mercy and love, and so He has given us *hope.* He knows what's going on in the world we live in and what we have to deal with every day. He knows what's going on inside of us, too. He knows we're imperfect and fallible. He knows that circumstances can gather round us like dark clouds, threatening to block out the light, choking and smothering us.

So hope is a gift from Him, an anchor for our souls in both stormy seas and calm waters (Hebrews 6:19).

And this God-given hope is not just a promise of a reward someday in a heavenly world, but it is also promises for *today*, a gift that affects and shapes our attitudes, perspective, and actions. Hope makes it possible for us to live today with joy, strength, and stamina.

The words from the book of Jeremiah quoted at the opening of this meditation are words from the Almighty Creator, describing what life will be like for those whose hope rests in Him. Read them again, and picture your life as a tree with roots reaching deep into the water...

Do you want to live like that? With stamina to keep going through the dry times. With strength enduring through desolate times. With your roots deep into a hope that is life-giving and productive. Do you long for the remainder of your days to be lived out in that way?

I do. I want a life just like that.

God says, *Yes, it can be so, even in this tumultuous world.*

ᵕᵕᵕᴛ WE HOPE IN A LIVING GOD ᴛᵕᵕᵕ

Now we live with great expectation... So be truly glad. There is wonderful joy ahead, even though you have to endure many trials for a little while.

– from 1 PETER 1:3, 6 –

Peter had recognized his friend Jesus as the Son of God. He had seen Jesus do things like walking on water and bringing people back from the dead. But when the pressure was on, he turned away and denied he even knew Jesus.

Peter certainly knew highs and lows of faith.

In the letters he later wrote to other believers, he made no bones about it—there would be trials and trouble in life. As a matter of fact, he wrote during a time when followers of Christ were being terrorized and killed. He had been arrested, beaten, and thrown in jail several times. But still, he wrote, *Live in expectation. There is wonderful joy ahead!*

How could Peter expect people to persevere? He knew how hard it can be. He had betrayed his close friend Jesus because he was afraid of the consequences. Had he since learned some secret that had changed him? What was this secret? How did he get to the place where he could say, *We live with great expectation?*

We need to know how to go on even when times are hard. We need to know how to look for joy.

Do we just have to grit our teeth and get through these hard times? What's the secret?

The book of Timothy has the answer for us: "because our hope is in the living God..." (see 1 Timothy 4:10).

Our hope is certain, not because we hope *for* but because we hope *in*. Our hope rests in a living God who cares deeply about His people and keeps His promises.

Moses, sent to lead the Israelite nation out of slavery in Egypt (no small job), was another man whose hope knew that the living God keeps His promises. In spite of the harsh and persistent opposition from the pharaoh of Egypt, Moses just kept right on going with God's plan—because "he kept his eyes on the one who is invisible" (Hebrews 11:27).

Where do our eyes go when we're looking for hope that holds joy and expectation? Only a living God can give us a hope like that—a hope that we know is certainty, no matter what is happening to us and around us.

If you do not believe in a living God, this book is probably not for you, although you're welcome to come along with us.

If you do believe in a living God, then keep your eyes on the one who is invisible.

I have no idea what situation you may be in today, but may I say this to you?

You *can* be glad. There is wonderful joy ahead!

·﹣,﹥⌒ WHY NOT? ⌒﹤,﹣·

Even when there was no reason for hope, Abraham kept hoping... He was fully convinced that God is able to do whatever He promises.

– **ROMANS 4:18, 21** –

If the foundation of our hope is that it resides in a *living* God, it is also just as important that we are convinced He is powerful enough to do what He says He will do.

Take Abraham. God promised him heirs as numerous as the stars in the sky. Abraham's wife laughed when she heard that. In their younger days, she had never been able to conceive; now they were both very old. Much too old to have a child. Their bodies were as good as dead, Abraham thought. Yet he believed what God told him. He is known as the father of those who believe.

And, exactly as God had promised, these two almost-dead bodies produced a son.

Abraham believed in "the God who brings the dead back to life and who creates new things out of nothing" (Romans 4:17). That's powerful. Dead back to life. New things out of *nothing.*

My life could use some of that power. How about yours?

If we believe in that living God, why not also believe that He can do even what sounds quite impossible?

Abraham did. Because Abraham knew his God and knew what his God could do. He never doubted.

And God did just what He said He would do.

The promises God gives us are for every step of our journey. We have a hope for easy times and hard, for joyful times, for the times we've failed and bungled things miserably, and for the times we feel powerless.

This is what our hope is built on—the promises God has made to His people who will believe Him.

Even when the world's logic scoffs that it is naïve and foolish to believe what God says, our hope still knows that we can trust what He tells us—because we believe in this living God, who does not lie and who can do what He says He will do.

Why not? Why not believe Him and take Him at His word? His promises are a gift to us, to give us an anchor for our souls as we walk through this world.

Why not hold onto an anchor that will keep steady through all of life?

Why not find out what God has for us?

ᴥᴥ᠇ᣔ ASK FOR THE GIFT ᣔᥱᥱᥱ᠌

Those who know your name trust in you, for you, O LORD,
do not abandon those who search for you.

– **PSALM 9:10** –

Dark times can make hope look impossible. What if we cannot seem to hold onto hope? We've all known times when we could not drag ourselves out of the pit, pull ourselves above the muck and the mud, and still hope.

Hope that enables us to trust and believe and stand steadfast comes as a gift from God.

In the times when we see no reason to hope and we cannot force hope to rise within, it is only the power of God's Spirit and the life-giving Word of God that can strengthen and encourage us and give us the gift of hope.

If not even a small, glowing ember of hope lives in your life right now, ask God to light a flame in you. Ask Him to give you that expectation of joy.

Read His Word; that's where He lays out His promises. Some of those promises are for the future—and aren't we all wondering what the future holds? Many more promises are for this very day. And you'll find that God's promises even cover your past!

To help us in our prayers for hope, I've included a prayer from the Psalms for each section, focusing on that section's particular hope. (You'll find them on the opening page of each section.) Most of these lines come from David, a man whose heart was in tune with God's. The prayers are short and simple, but they're wonderful to tuck away in memory and breathe as your own prayer when you need encouragement and help from the Heavenly Father.

He answers those prayers!

Remember that to God, hope is not just a wish. It is a sure thing. He *will* do what He says He will do. He gives us these bridges of hope so that we can go forward with confidence and in peace.

Listen to His voice speaking to you, and ask His Spirit to give you hope. Right now is a good time to do that.

He hears. He will answer your plea.

PRAY BOLDLY

Your word is my source of hope.
- **PSALM 119:114** -

King David must have been puzzled. He had a grand plan to build a beautiful temple, one fit for the LORD of the universe.

But God said, "No."

No?

David had been sure it was the right thing to do. It was the best way he knew to honor and worship God. But God had other plans. And at the same time He said *No*, He made David an astonishing promise (see 1 Chronicles 17).

God has made us some astonishing promises. He gives us this gift of hope through another great gift—His Word, the Holy Scriptures. There, God tells us what He is thinking, reminds us what He has done and will do, and gives us personal promises for every step of our earthly journeys.

Once David heard the new promise, he went to God in prayer.

"O, my God," prayed David, "I come to your throne boldly and confidently... because you have revealed your promise to me."

Yes, we can say that, too. As we look at God's promises about what He will do concerning our past and what He will do for us today and in the future, we can be bold in our prayers asking Him to fulfill those promises. We can say, "Father, You have said that You will do this; my hope knows that You will, and I depend on You!"

The Scriptures were written exactly for this purpose—to show us these bridges of hope that will carry us forward as we travel through life.

Romans 5:2 is part of the reason I went on my

search for *hope for today*. Do you know what it says? Paul wrote that because of our faith, Jesus Christ brought us into a place of undeserved privilege, where we can stand, confident and joyful.

What is included in this "undeserved privilege"? I wanted to know, so I embarked on my search. Much of the answer is outlined in Scripture, God's word to us. And, yes, the promises He's made to us do put us in an incredibly privileged place.

So we can be bold as we go to Him, because these are the words of a God who lives *now*,

who does not lie,

who can do what He says He can do,

and who *will* do what He says He will do.

Our faith can walk ahead, confident that the bridges of hope will carry us forward because they are *reality*.

To soak up more words of hope, see the appendix for a list of additional Scriptures.

PRAYER TO FOCUS OUR HOPE:

And so, LORD, where do I put my hope? My only hope is in you.

- PSALM 39:7 -

EVERYTHING WE NEED

❧ INCREDIBLE POWER ❧

*I also pray that you will understand the incredible
greatness of God's power for us who believe in him. This is
the same mighty power that raised Christ from the dead...*
- from **EPHESIANS 1:19, 20** -

I'm a grandma. Is that a good excuse for not
being tuned into modern-day superheroes?

So forgive my references to characters of
a past era. But more than one generation will
remember Superman, the man of steel, faster

than a speeding bullet, leaping tall buildings. (I do know that there's a modern version of Clark Kent.) And then there was a superhero in the '70s, an astronaut who had been rebuilt with bionic arms and legs and eye. Those super-dudes had every amazing capability needed to save the day when battling the bad guys. Today's superheroes have similar powers at their disposal, although their technology has advanced several decades.

Can you identify with any of those super characters? Oh. That's all fiction and comic books, right? *That's not reality*, you might be saying.

Maybe you can identify more closely with the disciple Peter. I know I do.

Peter, you remember, was the disciple who actually walked on water—briefly, until he panicked and sank into the waves. How often has fear or anxiety sunk our attempts to walk forward on faith?

Peter was the first to declare his belief that Jesus was the Son of God. This was a divine insight, surely. But then, under pressure, that same Peter deserted Jesus. Just turned and skedaddled, even though he had vowed to die with his friend, if necessary. Have we had like moments of failure, cowardice, or betrayal of the One we claim to love and follow?

Peter surely knew just as many miserable failures and mountaintop highs in his faith walk as we experience.

So it's remarkable to me that Peter later wrote those exuberant words: *We live with great expectation. There is wonderful joy ahead, even though...*

Even though.

Even though today looks grim.

Even though we're still battling some of our old thoughts and feelings.

Even though we are under attack.

Even though it seems that all our resources are exhausted.

Even though it looks as though the enemy is winning.

Maybe, a page or two back, you almost gave up reading this book and rejected as ridiculous the encouragement to be glad because there's joy ahead. Maybe you thought, *She has no idea what I'm going through.*

But it is the great God with incredible power who makes this promise to you, and *He* knows what you're going through.

And our hope knows that God keeps His promises.

Something happened to Peter, the up-again-down-again disciple. His life was changed by the power of the Spirit of God, and he became a great preacher, miracle-worker, and leader of the early church. He could write with firm hope that *there is wonderful joy ahead.*

When the divine power of God comes into a person's life, it changes things. This is a power of "incredible greatness." How great? Great enough to raise a man from the dead. With that kind of power, how could Peter's life remain the same?

Could that possibly happen in our lives? It's hard for us to imagine, isn't it? We believe that God's power raised Jesus from the dead; but... that kind of power making things happen in our lives?

Yes, that is the promise: The power of Almighty God is at work for those who believe in Him.

It's a greater power than any superhero has ever had. It goes beyond anything we can imagine.

Let's try this exercise: Think of the most difficult situation in your life right now.

Got something in mind?

Now, imagine what you think would be the most wonderful resolution of that situation. (Maybe the situation is so impossible that you can't even imagine how it might be resolved.)

Then, *know* that God has the power to do something far, far, far beyond what you've just imagined.

Does that light a longing in your soul?

Does it make you ask God to fire up that power in your life?

Take a moment to re-read the opening Scripture, and see who can have access to this power...

If we believe in Him, an incredibly great power is acting for us.

I want to know that kind of power in my life. How about you?

The "incredible greatness" of this power is difficult for us to comprehend, and we cannot explain exactly *how* it works. But God honors our faith, and the more we believe God and trust Him, the more we'll experience His power operating in our lives. We'll *see it.*

And even though we'll never plumb the depths of His power or even imagine what it might be like, He gives us glimpses of the greatness. Then every glimpse we have strengthens our certainty and cements our bridges of hope.

This is the promise we have for today: Divine power is at work in the lives of those who believe God, whether we *feel* it or not.

And I know that if we want to see more of

that power, God hears and answers the prayer of, *Father, help my unbelief.*

✦ HE CAN AND HE WILL ✦

By his divine power, God has given us everything we need for living a godly life.
– from 2 PETER 1:3 –

We've all had days when we've been faced with something we think is impossible, and we have no idea how we're going to cope with it.

When we're inadequate and overwhelmed and God says that He will supply everything we need, can we believe Him?

Behind this promise are two truths: He is *able* to supply our every need. And He is *willing.*

He is able. To me, getting through today might look impossible. But it's not impossible for God. Remember? *Incredible, divine power. Strong enough to raise the dead, to bring something out of nothing.* I can't imagine what that kind of power will look like in my life, but if it's available to me, I certainly want to find out!

He is also willing. Scripture tells us over and over again that we're to bring all our anxieties and concerns to God because He is concerned about every little detail of our lives—and He will take care of us (and our little details). Jesus said that our Heavenly Father knows what we need before we even ask for it (see Matthew 6:8). He is often compared to a shepherd who sees to every need of his flock.

Consider this: If the God of the universe cared so much about us that He was willing to become a human like us and put Himself through terrible humiliation and an ugly death so that He could adopt us into His family and we could have a good relationship with Him, then don't you suppose He will care for us, tenderly supplying what we need, constantly watching over us, and leading us along the path that will bring us finally home to Him?

He does exactly that. He rescued you from the kingdom of darkness. He paid a huge price for you, my friend, and now He's promised to supply everything you need on your journey home. Everything.

A GODLY LIFE

By his divine power, God has given us everything we need for living a godly life.

– from 2 PETER 1:3 –

Maybe the phrase that jumped out at you in the opening verse from 2 Peter wasn't *everything we need.* Maybe you couldn't grasp the enormity of that promise because you are troubled by that phrase *godly life.*

Are you thinking that your life is far from godly, and therefore this promise may not be one that you can claim—because you aren't "good enough"?

I am a freelance writer. I make my living by writing, editing, and helping people publish their books. When I see an interesting scene, my mind begins to think of words and phrases to describe that scene to evoke the image in the mind of a reader. Tastes, smells, sounds, feelings often prompt me to tinker with words, trying to capture sensations in phrases. I study the writing of others. I write something almost every day, even if it is just my own prayer or a journal entry. If, for some reason, I'm away from my keyboard for several days, I feel a hunger to get back to the sound and feel of the keys as I see my thoughts taking shape in black and white on the screen.

But, you know what? It wasn't too long ago that I found it difficult to say "I am a writer." After all, I was just starting out in this life. I didn't have the experience or expertise displayed by far better writers. I would compare something I had written with the paragraphs of a writer I admired and think, *Why did I ever imagine that I could do this?* In my circle of family and friends, no one had ever done this for a living.

But my choice to pursue this path has shaped the landscape of my thoughts, my schedule, and my actions. I *am* a writer. Not always a good writer. Not the writer I'd like to be. But on the journey of becoming a better writer. I know I still have much to learn, practice, and master.

If you are living a godly life, you might be described in a similar way. You might hesitate to label yourself *godly*, but...

You know the Almighty God reigns in the heavens. You reverence Him and worship who He is. You seek to know Him better and to understand how He would have His people live. The landscape of your thoughts, actions, and choices are affected by your awareness and respect for the living God and His standards. You don't always think and act accordingly, but even your regret or disappointment at your own less-than-desirable actions reflect your desire to be a person who is molded by God.

And that is the best way this writer knows to describe a "godly life."

The apostle Paul wrote a letter to a young pastor, Timothy, and talked of "training" for godliness. It is a daily thing, this training of our thoughts and actions, much like training of the body for particular endeavors. But, Paul wrote, "Physical training is good, but training for godliness is much better, promising benefits in this life and in the life to come" (1 Timothy 4:8).

Just as we're all at different places in our physical conditioning, we're all at different places in our godliness training. But we have chosen this godly path, we're devoted to it, and we practice shaping our lives accordingly.

"Godly lives" are not perfect lives. If that were possible, you and I would have no need to hear the promises of God about forgiveness and mercy; we would have no reason to learn to repent and confess and ask for cleansing; we would not need the assurance that He will supply what we need, today, to live this life.

But He *has* made that promise. We can depend on it. Our faith can move forward over that bridge, confident that God *can* and *will* do what He says He will do and will supply everything we need.

Doesn't that change everything? Doesn't that make the journey exciting?

Yes, we can live with great expectation!

ᴖᴖᴖ COMING TO KNOW HIM ᴖᴖᴖ

By his divine power, God has given us everything we need
for living a godly life. We have received all of this by
coming to know him.
– from **2 PETER 1:3** –

The apostle Paul once preached a sermon in a city that believed in dozens of deities. You probably remember the stories of gods and goddesses that Greek mythology created in an attempt to explain the universe and human nature. I find it interesting, though, that apparently the citizens of this town still felt there must be something or someone *more.* They had erected an altar dedicated to "The Unknown God."

Paul proceeded to tell them who this unknown God was: The Creator, the Lord of the universe, the Only God. God's purpose, said Paul, was that men and women would seek Him and come to know Him.

We hear this message throughout the Old Testament: God says, again and again, *I want you to know me. I want it more than rituals of worship* (Hosea 6:6). *If you seek me, you'll find me.* (Jeremiah 29:13 and Isaiah 45:19). And, *I am waiting to help you.*

The Creator wants to re-establish a relationship with men and women. He wants to bring them into His family as His sons and daughters and give them the life they were meant to have in the beginning. He wants to supply all we need to have that life.

Did you notice in the opening verse that it now includes more of the Scripture? It answers the question of *how* this bounty of resources comes into our lives—

By coming to know Him.

When we come to know Him and believe in Him, He adopts us as His children and we have available all the resources of heaven and the King of heaven!

That sounds so simple, doesn't it? But how do we learn to know God? Dare we be so presumptuous to claim to know the Almighty, Supreme God? How can our minds begin to understand who and what He is?

God has provided answers for those questions, too.

One way we learn to know Him is through the Scriptures—the Word He has given us. We'll devote an entire section to that in just a few pages.

Another way we learn to know God is by learning to know Jesus, who was God coming as a flesh-and-blood human being to the world. Jesus called Himself the "stairway to heaven" and is the supreme bridge God has given us.

And a third way is through the Holy Spirit. To everyone who believes in Jesus, God gives the right to become a son or daughter of God, and to everyone who becomes His child, God gives His own Spirit (John 1:12 and Romans 8:15).

God "gives" us His Spirit. His own Spirit "lives" in us. That's a mystery too deep for me to even try to understand or explain. But that's what God says happens within those who believe! And one of the things the Spirit does is teach us about God the Father. It is a spiritual connection we have to Him, and through which we learn to know Him better.

Think of the phrase "kindred spirits," a phrase we use to describe the connection two people might have, understanding each other on a special level. The connection we have been given to our Creator is even greater. Paul wrote that the Spirit shows us God's thinking and His "secrets"— things we have not seen or known before. That amazes me! (See 1 Corinthians 2:10-12).

As we ponder each thing we need to get through today, we'll see that Jesus Christ and His Spirit within us are the secret to everything. Because we do have those connections to the Almighty God, our hope can live with great expectation.

✢✦✧ JESUS, THE SAVIOR ✧✦✢

The Father sent his Son to be the Savior of the world.

— from 1 JOHN 4:14 —

I am so glad you're reading this first line. I hope you will go on to the next, and the next.

Because that means you have not been deterred by the title.

Some will look at that title and think, *I know all about Jesus the Savior. I don't need a review of this.*

But I don't know all about the Savior. I keep seeing more and more of Him. I hope you do, too. And if we are asking *How will I get through today?*, the answer is *the Savior*.

✢✦✧

The first thing we want to do is get a fresh look at the word *savior.*

I've heard that word in church and Christian conversations so often that I'm afraid its meaning has become dulled. It's part of the lingo that slips so easily off Christian tongues but possibly never penetrates our brains and hearts. Let's change that!

First, before we even think of Scripture, let's go to our secular dictionaries. Most versions will define *savior* as a person who delivers or keeps one from peril or injury. A savior *rescues.* Think about how you use this word and its various forms in a secular sense: "Whew. I was so happy to see you. You saved me..." Or, "That job offer came at just the right time. It was my salvation."

Salvation is rescue. A savior rescues.

Then we look at the Hebrew word for salvation and *save.* The "Word Study System" of my Tyndale Bible defines *Yeshu'ah* and *yasha'* as "removing an object from a dangerous situation or the state of being delivered from distress." In the New Testament, the Greek word we have translated as savior is *sōtēr,* meaning "a person who rescues or delivers another from a dangerous circumstance."

All of that to say that my relationship to Jesus changed dramatically when I began to see that He is the Savior who will rescue me... on a daily basis and on into forever and ever.

It has helped me so much to replace *save* and *savior* with *rescue* and *rescuer.*

I needed Jesus to save me from the punishment of hell. That's why I first came to Him—because I was scared of what would happen after I died. Like me, many people are thinking only of a way to avoid punishment and hell when they use the word *Savior.* But Jesus the *Savior* did not come to earth only to provide a way for people to avoid the punishment we deserve. He did come to do that, yes. But He came to rescue us from so much more.

Jesus Christ came to help us. Because we needed help. Help in dealing with our past. Help to face today and to live with joy and without fear. And help to walk confidently into the future.

Humans were created in the image of God! We so easily forget that, but it was the Plan of the Creator.

And then, we spoiled it.

Jesus comes into our lives to re-establish our relationship with God. That's the overarching history of our race—and it's our own personal history. We are not what God originally created humans to be, but Jesus came *to help us be what God intended.* He stepped into our history to rescue us from hopelessness and put us back on track in the Plan, so to speak.

Jesus Christ rescues us from the disease of sin. Sin is anything other than God's good plan for life, and we've all been infected with it since the Garden of Eden. Jesus rescues me from the power of that disease. He is changing me, helping me escape the slavery to the old selfishness and stubbornness that resisted and rebelled against God's standards. He is changing my character. He is helping me grow into my new status as a child of God.

Jesus rescues us from the prison of our guilt and from the penalty for our sinfulness. The freedom Jesus Christ offers is available to anyone who believes in His message.

He rescued us from the clutches of the fear of death. To those who believe, He gives immortality. Let the weight of those words settle into your soul. Death is not the end. There's a phrase in the book of Hebrews that has captured my imagination. It refers to Jesus, and His mission of reconnecting us to God, by "the power of a life that cannot be destroyed." I've been pondering that phrase because—amazing!—those who belong to Him share in that same life and power. How does that change your perspective if you know you're living a *life that cannot be destroyed?*

The phrase *Jesus saves* might be worn out with use. It floats past our ears and we miss the power of it. However, *Jesus rescues!* is a forceful reminder for me. Jesus was on a rescue mission when He died to tear away the barrier between me and God and to put me on a track to a different destiny.

That makes our future look anything but hopeless.

But what about today? How does Jesus rescue us today? Galatians 1:4 tells us that Jesus gave His life, just as God planned, "in order to rescue us from this evil world in which we live." That is rescue today, right now, friends! Those who believe are living in a place of great privilege and will have everything they need to live out their lives as children of God. That's what we are going to celebrate in these pages.

When Jesus was speaking a parable about being sent from God, He referred to a line from the psalms: "This is the LORD's doing, and it is wonderful to see" (Psalm 118:23). This is God's doing—sending a rescuer to our world! It is indeed a wonderful thing.

A HELPER FOREVER

"And I will ask the Father, and he will give you another Helper, to be with you forever."

- JOHN 14:16 ESV -

Have you ever tried to imagine yourself as one of the twelve in Jesus' closest circle of disciples?

Their decision to follow this man must have caused disruption in their family and occupational lives—and not just bumps in family life, but great earthquakes of upheaval. The fishermen left the tending of nets and boats to their business partners. Matthew walked away from his profitable job. They soon became all too aware that the religious authorities they had lived under all their lives were sternly opposed, even hostile toward Jesus. They knew even Jesus' family questioned His sanity. At first, people eagerly flocked to hear this new teacher, but once they heard certain parts of His teaching, many in the crowd started shaking their heads, calling Him a troublemaker.

For those twelve men, I'm sure, the decision to follow Jesus was a choice that brought conflict and challenges into their personal lives. Yet they stayed committed to their choice, believing that He was leading them along a new path that was more important than anything in their old life.

Then one night, He told them He would soon be leaving this earth.

And as Jesus talked, He wasn't at all encouraging with these words: "Here on Earth, you are going to have troubles and sorrows."

Oh! They had looked to Him to fulfill all the wonderful promises God had given their people generations before. They had been sure that this Jesus was the Promised One who would usher in a wonderful new era for their people. They had thought He was the Savior, their Rescuer, their new King.

But now He was disappearing from their lives and leaving them here in this world of trouble and sorrow.

Can you imagine their dismay?

We don't have to imagine. We are in much the same situation. We have decided to follow Jesus. That means we have some difficult changes to make. Our perspective changes. Our values change. Our choices change. We face resistance and hostility from those around us who do not share our belief. We were not whisked off to heaven in a chariot as soon as we believed, but we were left here, right in the middle of a world of trouble and sorrow.

Let's move on from those words of *trouble and sorrow* and go quickly to the rest of Jesus' statement: "But take heart," our King says, "because I have overcome the world."

Now, what does *that* mean?

We already know what the disciples would only learn later: We know that Jesus died, that God's power raised Him from the dead, that He is alive today. We know that He holds all power and authority. But how does He help us today?

How can we take heart when we have trouble and sorrow in this world?

That is what we will meditate on in this book, but there are even better pages to read to encourage your heart. Read John's book, chapters 14 through 17. These are Jesus' words to the disciples He left on this earth. They are words for us, too—words encouraging us to stay close to Him and trust Him, words of assurance about the future, words He spoke so that we would have peace. Chapter 17 includes His prayer to the heavenly Father, in which He prayed for you and me!

And throughout these four chapters, we hear Jesus repeat, again and again, a promise to His disciples in every generation: "I will send you a Helper."

"My spirit will be with you."

Have you heard that? Has someone said it to you?

It's most often uttered as an expression of empathy and support, yet even on that casual, worldly level, people express a hint of belief that there is a power behind our physical presence and resources.

Christians believe in a similar expression that is a mystery we cannot explain—and it sounds ridiculous to those who do not believe.

Jesus said, "My Spirit will live in you."

Not *be with you*, but *live in you!* The Spirit of God!

Already, you may be hesitating, drawing back from making such a claim. Our minds find this truth hard to grasp. It sounds radical, extreme, even boastful to believe such a thing. But this is what God says: His Spirit lives in everyone who believes.

Every believer since Jesus lived on this earth has been given the same Helper He promised His disciples. We know this Helper as the Holy Spirit, or the Spirit of Christ, or the Spirit of God. The three are all one. I can't explain the Trinity of our God. But Jesus said that He and the Father would come and live with those who believe, and that is in the person of the Holy Spirit within us.

Jesus' words were far more than a catchphrase as He said goodbye. This is God's reality—that He comes and lives in His children. And it is His Spirit who births something new in us: a new heart, a new character, a new life. It is the Spirit who reminds us what Jesus taught and also leads us to truths and insights for our lives. It is the Spirit who gives us divine strength and power— beyond any resources of our own. It is the Spirit who somehow teaches us to know God. It is the Spirit who brings comfort and hope.

It is the Spirit who keeps us connected to Christ from whom we draw *His* life and power. That's the power that overcomes the world. We'll see this in every section of this book. Jesus is alive, His Spirit is in us, and He is working, saving, rescuing, and creating—in every moment of today. That is why we can hold onto hope.

As we go forward and seek answers to our questions about getting through today, we look always to God, our Father; to Jesus, the Rescuer; and to the Spirit, our Helper. God doesn't leave us alone to muddle through life. Hope knows that He is right here with us, working with divine, incredible power in every circumstance of our lives.

"LET'S BE REALISTIC"

Since you have been raised to new life with Christ, set your sights on the realities of heaven.

- from COLOSSIANS 3:1 -

"Once you do this, your life will never be the same."

I think I first heard those words from my dad, who spoke them to me when, as a college student, I bought my first car.

He was referring to the ongoing care and cost of owning a car. I admitted that he was probably right (although I had yet to learn it by practical living and a drain on my savings), but I was thinking more of how this new independence would change my life. At the time, we were a family of six drivers, sharing one car.

Perhaps that memory stays with me because I've learned, throughout decades since, that life brings many changes in circumstances and status. And with each, we are faced with new *realities.*

A single woman weds, and adjusts to the realities of sharing everything with another person. Couples have children, and their lives take on new realities. A student graduates, and his daily life is suddenly filled with both new opportunities and new responsibilities.

Since that day I bought a car, my life has changed, in many ways and over many seasons. With each change, the realities of my daily life changed. The most dramatic and precious change I've known is when I realized that God had taken me in as His own child.

When we come to Christ, God says He does away with the old: "The old is gone, the new has come" (2 Corinthians 5:17). We are living a new life.

We have a *new existence* in a realm that goes beyond the limits and boundaries of this earthly world. The letter of Ephesians tells us that we have now been "seated in the heavenly realms." What can that mean?

It's something like our metaphors of "getting a piece of the pie" or "having a seat at the table." God's metaphor, though, goes beyond anything we know on this earth. He has placed our feet (another metaphor) in the kingdom of His realities. He has adopted us as His children. We are already in a place where we have the privilege of partaking of the blessings of heaven. We still must live a life in this world, but we can *already* live by the realities of the Kingdom of Heaven. We are not bound by this world's "realities."

The apostle Paul writes of this in Colossians 3. Through Christ, you have a new life, established in the heavenly realms, Paul wrote. So "set your sights on the realities of heaven."

I am often prodded by this question: *Where have you set your sights?* On the boundaries of earth? Have we limited our sights to what our culture would declare possible, practical, logical, or sensible? Or do we set our sights on God's truth? Do we go to Him to find what is possible? Do we look to Him for limits and standards, potential and power? Do we live in His realities?

Are we short-sighted, keeping our eyes at earth-level? Or are we heaven-sighted, keeping our eyes on the eternal unseen?

"Mom, when you walk like that—with your eyes on the ground—you miss all the great things about taking a walk," my daughter said to me one day when we were out for a walk.

She was right, of course. My eyes were glued to the ground because I was in a contest. For a year, a friend and I picked up all the coins we came across in stores, parking lots, on sidewalks or roadsides, in airports, or anywhere that coins drop unnoticed. (We'd find money in surprising and strange places.) On New Year's Eve, we would count our coins to see who had the larger stash.

But I was missing the beautiful sky, the summer flowers, the friendly greetings, the interesting vignettes of life we passed. I wasn't even giving full attention to the conversation with my daughter. Hoping for a paltry penny or two, I was missing all the richness of that day.

That's what happens when our eyes are only "on the ground." If we never lift our sight to heavenly realities *in which we now live,* we're settling for paltry pennies, when we could be having our breath taken away by the riches that are now ours.

When one becomes a mother, suddenly all of life is seen through the eyes of a mother and responded to from the mind and heart of a mother. The owner of a company makes day-to-day decisions from the perspective of ownership; an employee of the same company works from a different point-of-view. Our thinking changes whenever we experience a change in status: A junior-high student moves on to high school; a single person marries or a married person loses their spouse; a person is elected to a position in a church congregation. All such changes are catalysts for adjustments in our thoughts and actions. We see things differently because of our change of status.

In Colossians 3, Paul went on to encourage us to "think about the things of heaven, not the things of earth." That does not mean that we must focus only on some future day when we are given a life in heaven and we ignore the joys and hardships, details and responsibilities, of our lives on earth. It does mean, though, that we see this earthly life through the filter of heaven's values, priorities, and laws.

We've had a change of status. We're now "seated in heavenly places." We already have access to heavenly blessings, as citizens of heaven and children of God.

We live in heaven's realities, even while we're still breathing earth's air. In this, our new life, we must learn to think and act according to heaven's realities.

It's worth reading a bit further in Colossians 3. Verse 3 says that we have died to this earthly life. Our *real life* is "hidden with Christ in God."

This life we're living in the heavenly realm might not be as readily apparent as earthly things we can touch and hear and see, but it exists and it is real. Just as Christ is hidden from our sight now but is alive and real and active, so we are already alive in a hidden, heavenly life. And someday, when Christ is revealed to the whole world, then we will also know in full what our real life is like.

In the meantime, Paul wrote, we should live lives here that are befitting the children of God and citizens of heaven. He gave concrete guidelines to put to death the old, sinful things that are "lurking" inside you (I understand that word "lurking"!) and put on your new nature that has been birthed in you by the Spirit of Christ.

We know, though, that new status alone cannot be counted on to generate appropriate new thoughts and new actions. New parents need time to grow into their new roles. An employee promoted to manager needs to learn new ways of relating to those he now supervises. A teenager gaining her driver's license must learn to think differently on the highway than a passenger. And a teenager buying a car also learns about new realities—along with an independence, there's also maintenance, insurance, tires, and gas.

In the same way, this learning to live in heaven's realities is a maturing thing. So is leaving the old nature behind and putting on the new nature. The more we work at this, the more we will "grow up" into fully living in heavenly realities and realms. We mature as children of the heavenly Father.

May these pages encourage you as you learn to live in the heavenly realms where Christ has placed you, in *God's* realities that your hope can depend on and live by.

EVERY LITTLE THING WE NEED

The LORD directs the steps of the godly. He delights in every detail of their lives.

- **PSALM 37:23** -

Crocuses arrive at just the right time in spring. If God has favorites, surely the crocus must be one of His favorite flowers.

I have long thought that God planned for this tiny little flower to bloom just as winter departs and spring arrives, because if crocuses came along in July, their delicate melody would be drowned out by the boisterous shouting of tall and robust perennials. No one would notice little purple, white, and pink clusters fighting for space among the drifts of mid-summer lilies. In March or April, though, against the bare ground or sometimes poking their colors above the snow like flags of hope, crocuses are celebrated and cherished.

As I write this, the purple crocus along my sidewalk arrived—once again in perfect timing. It sent a breath of hope and newness and cheer into my week, just when I needed it.

Do you notice all those things that arrive at just the right time, just when you need them? A call from a friend, a sunny day, a devotional or a Scripture, a hug, an affirming word, the sudden memory of where you put your car keys, an out-of-the-blue reminder of something important that you had forgotten.

You might be wondering why we're even taking the time and pages to consider those "little" things in life.

I just want to go on record as declaring my firm belief that these small coincidences are not chance at all—they are gifts from our heavenly Father, who knows just what we need. Psalm 37:23 says that God delights in *every detail* of our lives. James wrote that every good gift is from Him (James 1:17). And in one of the apostle Paul's sermons, he said that even instances of joy in the hearts of unbelievers is evidence of God's goodness (Acts 14:17).

Even some of those things that seem to "go wrong" turn out to bear gifts. We might often be frustrated or disappointed by a situation, but later we see that good has resulted from it. God's gifts are sometimes packaged in ways we would never expect.

Heaven's reality is that God *does* care about every little thing in our lives, all the small stuff, those little things that some would say are too insignificant for Him to bother with. Many of my prayers have concerned small things—not only giving thanks for the gifts, but asking, *Shall I call her now? Help me resist eating four cookies. I need a cheerful word from a friend to keep me going. Help me make time in my schedule to take a walk today. I really need a good night's sleep.*

Small things. But I will say it one more time—I firmly believe that God *does* bother with all those little things we need.

We're going to talk about many *big* things

that we need to get through every day, but at the same time, watch for the gifts of God's love, coming every day, supplying what you need, even in the small stuff.

‿ᴧᴧ᷄ MAKING IT PERSONAL ᴧᴧ᷄‿

And so, Lord, where do I put my hope?
My only hope is in you.
– PSALM 39:7 –

It took me more than a year to put it together. Sometimes, my slow-wittedness astounds me.

I have a friend who has frequently said that she doesn't hang all her hopes on a person or a thing. "My expectations are only from Him," she declares.

When she first said this to me, I thought I understood what she was saying. When we place all our hope on another person, an organization, system, or any earthly entity, we open the door to frustration and disappointment and bitterness and anger.

It took me a while, though, to realize that this is exactly what Scriptures were also saying. *Hope* is *expectation*, so when we say "You alone are my hope, O Lord," we are placing our expectations on Him—and nowhere else.

Nowhere else!

You may have seen the connection at once. It took me a while. But when it finally hit me, it shook and rearranged my thinking and my praying.

Ponder this: If God says He will supply *everything we need,* and if our hope in that promise can be a sure expectation, then that means we can look to Him to fill all our needs in:

- finances
- wisdom
- health
- friendships
- comfort
- security
- safety
- strength

Oh, the list could go on and on. But here's the question I ask myself: What expectation, what *hopes* do I have today? What or who am I counting on to have those hopes fulfilled?

For example, in finances and security—am I counting on my ability to work and my retirement fund? Is that the one thing I am trusting to ensure that I have what I need? Are my retirement savings the "god" that protects my future? What about wisdom? Where do I go *first* when I'm wrangling with a tough decision? Who do I look to for guidance on the "best way" for my life?

I believe there's only one place we can rest all—yes, *all*—our hopes and know that what we need will be supplied. That one place is in our almighty and loving Father.

He has said He will supply *everything* we need to get through today as His children and partners in Christ's mission—and that would cover every area of our lives.

Our lives and futures are in our Heavenly Father's hands, and James reminds us that all good things are gifts from Him (Psalm 31:15, James 1:17).

As you go forward through these pages, there may be statements you find extreme, perhaps even disturbing. I hope so. I hope the current boundaries of our trust in God are pushed out as we look at His promises together. I hope our view of our lives is shaken. I hope every page increases our desire to live in God's realities.

Our Psalm prayer with this section helps us refocus our expectations and place them in the one sure and dependable Person. Take a minute to go back and review that prayer.

God is faithful. He is committed to every generation of His people, and His blessing is on all those who trust in Him (Psalm 119:90, Jeremiah 17:7).

He does not forget us. His love surrounds us. His incredible power works for His children.

Surely there is no better place to put all our expectations as we face today.

FROM ANOTHER PERSPECTIVE

God has given each of you a gift from his great variety of spiritual gifts. Use them well to serve one another.

– **1 PETER 4:10** –

I have to sneak a few more paragraphs into this section, because I think there's another aspect of this hope of God supplying what we need. And it's important.

Paul wrote a letter to the new Christians in the large and prosperous city of Corinth. This was a church he had founded in a city that bore diverse religious influences. Geographically, Corinth was in Greece, but in Paul's day, it was likely part of the Roman Empire and under considerable Roman influence. There may have also been Egyptian influence there, as well, in the various religious cults.

Paul knew these people well; he had founded the church there and lived and worked in Corinth for more than a year. Then he moved on, but he later wrote this letter to address all kinds of issues the church was having. They had a ton of problems, and most of them were very messy. Even non-church people, Paul wrote, would be appalled at some of what was going on in the Corinth church at that time.

Yet Paul began his letter by addressing these people as those "called by God to be his own holy people."

They were far from perfect, burdened still by many pagan ideas and influences, selfish, and argumentative.

Does that sound familiar? It sounds like my life. So far from the mark, it seems. Still struggling with so many things...

And it sounds like my church: Still working at understanding what it means to be God's holy people, and then trying to live that out.

Paul wrote to those so-much-less-than-perfect Corinthians,

> Now you have every spiritual gift you
> need as you eagerly wait for the return of
> our LORD Jesus Christ. He will keep you
> strong to the end so that you will be free
> from all blame on the day when our LORD
> Jesus Christ returns. God will do this, for
> he is faithful to do what he says, and he
> has invited you into partnership with his

Son, Jesus Christ our LORD. (1 Corinthians 1:7-9)

Can you imagine what the people in that church must have felt as they opened Paul's letter and began reading?

They were well aware of all the *unholy* stuff going on; probably every person was embroiled in one or two of the specific problems Paul will go on to discuss in the letter.

Yet the first thought he brings to them is that God has invited them to a new kind of life, He supplies everything necessary to live that life, and He intends to eventually bring His people to the end of this age... blameless!

How would you feel, reading such an assurance, especially knowing the trouble that churns through your church? And, perhaps, even knowing that you have played a part in all those problems?

The next time you're in church or in a Bible study or any kind of function of your church, look around at the people next to you.

God has placed each of us where we are for a reason. He has said we are now His representatives and partners in Christ's mission. That mission is given us not only as we go into the world, but also as we live with our brothers and sisters in the family of God.

The Spirit of Christ connects all of God's people. He created this connection for the good of each one of us—so that we grow more and more like Him, *together.*

This connection is meant to give us strength and knowledge and to help us grow up in our faith and love and hope.

He makes the whole body fit together perfectly. As each part does its own special work, it helps the other parts grow, so that the whole body is healthy and growing and full of love.
(Ephesians 4:16)

In other words, each one of us has been given a part to play in supplying what other followers of Christ need.

Sometimes God supplies what we need through other parts of Christ's body. Sometimes, God uses you to supply what a sister or brother in God's family is in need of at a particular time.

This is not limited to the congregation you'll sit in on Sunday morning. It applies to your relationship with coworkers who also follow Jesus; to your online networks with other Christians; to both your closest friendships and your casual encounters in everyday life.

Each one of us is called to a special ministry to every other child of God.

> God has given each of you a gift from his great variety of spiritual gifts. **Use them well to serve one another**... Do it with all the strength and energy that God supplies. Then everything you do will bring glory to God through Jesus Christ. (from 1 Peter 4:10,11, my emphasis added)

I read the assurance that God gives gifts to His family so that we can help each other, but at the same time, I know too well how less-than-perfect my own life is, how often I stumble and need help on my pilgrimage, how many times I open the door to doubt or discouragement or guilt over the unholy still in my life.

And given all that, how could I possibly be of service to others and help others to grow?

I hear Jesus' words: *I have called you to a new life, and I will supply everything you need to stand strong. Stay close to Me. I am the one who will get you through. And in the end, you will stand blameless!*

God will do this, Paul declares. He has invited you to be His partner in His work here on earth, and He will supply everything you need to do that.

He will do it, because He keeps His promises.

Christ's church—the Spirit connection we have with every other child of God—is a special supply line that God has set up. Each one of us is part of that supply line. It's one way He provides what we need as we live out our mission.

For more assurance that God will supply all you need, see the appendix for a list of additional Scriptures.

PRAYER WHILE YOU'RE WAITING:

I am worn out waiting for your

rescue, but I have put my hope in

your word.

– **PSALM 119:81** –

PROMISES FOR THOSE WHO WAIT

WORN OUT WITH WAITING?

Be strong, and let your heart take courage, all you who wait for the LORD!

— PSALM 31:24 —

A number of years ago, I wrote an online article about patience and endurance. I'd been inspired that week by spending a sunny afternoon with my young grandson, planting seeds on barren ground. Scattering handfuls of seeds, we left them to soak up sun and water, as we dreamed of the sea of wildflowers we would have the next summer.

Guess what?

We never saw one blossom.

The area where we scattered seeds in hope was filled over with dirt later that summer and then planted with new grass. Any seedlings that managed to persist and survive would have been mowed down every week for the past six years.

What happens to our hope when it seems to be repeatedly mowed down before we see a blossom?

What if we move forward in hope over God's bridges of promise and find the road still goes on and on and on? Or if we plant seeds in hope and then *years go by* and what we confidently expected has not yet come to pass?

What if we're depending on a promise God has made us—but we don't see that promise fulfilled?

What if, like the writer of songs in Psalms, we are asking God, "How long, Lord, *how long?*"

We know His timing is not our timing. We know His plan is usually quite different and always far better than ours.

Sometimes, though, we do grow weary. Sometimes, we do want to give it up. Sometimes, we bristle with anger and ask Him, *Why haven't you...?*

We need to know His promises. That's what our hope is built on. His promises are, indeed, our only hope.

So while we wait for Him to act, we'll focus on His promises for those who wait.

✣ WAITING IN HIS PRESENCE ✣

All day long I put my hope in you.
- from **PSALM 25:5** -

I'm doubting my choice. It could be that I mistitled this section.

Is *wait* a word that is no longer meaningful? Has it become too old-fashioned? Too counter-culture? We are a fast-food, fast-turnaround, fast-everything society.

Oh, but wait.

We do have a meaningful new phrase in today's slang: *"Wait for it..."*

Does that indicate that we do still know the meaning of *wait?*

I don't think so. After all, even that new phrase has reduced the meaning of *wait* to *"hold on for just a few seconds, it's coming."*

And those who wait on the Lord often have to hold on and wait longer than a few seconds.

Are you waiting on the Lord for something? What does *waiting* mean to you?

Let's look at the original Hebrew and Greek of the Bible again. In both languages, several words have been translated into our English word *wait.* The original words all carry a confidence that something *will* come to pass. Their meaning also implies a "seeing" or "watching" of something that is coming. They all hold *expectation.*

And so we're right back to our definition of hope. We live in great expectation. We hope. We wait. Because we *know* it will come to pass. Our eyes of faith can see it.

On second thought, maybe that popular phrase "Wait for it..." is a good mantra for children of God. Because it tells you: *Yes, you can depend on this. The fulfillment of His promise is definitely coming. Wait for it.*

We have wonderful and comforting promises from God for those who wait.

But we all know that it is often difficult to wait.

I've chosen the Psalm prayer for this section because it's one I need as I wait. I often want to complain to God: "My hope is slipping away. I'm worn out by waiting, and I'm just holding on by my fingernails. Why does this go on so long?

Why don't You do something *now?"*

At those times, the enemy—with glee, I imagine—slips in and starts to drop sly hints of doubt into my thoughts. I need something to counteract those doubts.

So how do we hang in there? How do we hold on to our hope? How do we pray the last half of that prayer (on the title page of this section) that declares, in spite of everything, that we still believe the promises and wait in great expectation?

Willpower will not keep us in the race. Willpower is too easily convinced to quit. We cannot hold onto our hope if it all depends on our own resources.

The only thing that keeps us hanging in there is if we hang onto the Vine.

Patience (and waiting) is one of the fruits of Christ's Spirit living in us. Christ says that He is the Vine, and when the Vine's life flows into the branch (me), He gives me the power to wait. When I hold onto the Vine, *He holds me.*

David knew the importance of staying connected to the One who gives life. He wrote Psalm 37, chock full of promises for God's people. But I think this line from that psalm holds the key:

Be still in the presence of the LORD, and wait patiently for him to act. (Psalm 37:7)

There's our answer—*in the presence of the Lord.* We simply must stay in His presence. Don't look around. Don't wander off. Don't let go!

When my hope is slipping, when I start doubting, it's because I've spent too little time in His presence.

Oh, I know, God is always present with me. Scripture assures us of that. But I am not always present with Him. I go wandering off, too often and too far.

Again, David gives us a good model. In Psalm 25:5 he writes: "All day long I put my hope in you."

What picture does that create for you? I see someone who throughout the day consciously, consistently, and repeatedly comes to God and hands their hope over to Him.

Here, Lord, is my hope. I am placing my hopes and expectations—for everything I need—in You and you alone.

Not just once, but continually, all day long, staying in His presence.

It's the only way we'll be able to wait.

✦ THE VOICE OF SOMEONE ✦
WHO LOVES YOU

The LORD is good to those who depend on Him.
— from **LAMENTATIONS 3:25** —

At times, our hearts need to hear the voice of someone who we know loves us no matter what. You know those times—when you have to talk to your sister or your spouse or your friend, not because they have answers, but because you know they care about you.

Just so with the children of God.

Waiting on God to act can, in itself, be a trial, a test of our endurance. While we wait, we are prodded by doubt, frustration, and questioning. We're even tempted to idolatry, tempted to go to someone or something other than God to give us answers, to help us, and to save the situation and rescue us.

As we wait, we need to hear the voice of Someone who loves us.

What do we wait for? Everything. Sometimes we wait for guidance in a personal dilemma. We wait for Him to act in a situation. We wait for Him to change us. We wait for good things to emerge from hard places. We wait for hearts of stone to change. We wait for a cloud of grief to lift. We wait.

We wait for the fulfillment of the promises God has made to us. We depend on Him to keep His word.

Sometimes God acts quickly. Sometimes, we think He is much too slow.

As we wait, the one thing that will comfort and assure us is hearing His voice.

So we search His words. Here are some of my favorites. These passages speak peace into my soul when I do not yet have answers, when I'm feeling tossed about by doubt or frustration, or when, like the psalmist, I wonder why God doesn't *do something now*. These reassurances help me to stay at peace while waiting, because I pray and wait on the God described here:

- He watches over me with unfailing love. (Psalm 33:18, 19)

- He is good to those who depend on Him. (Lamentations 3:25)

- When I come to Him, He shows me love and compassion. (Isaiah 30:18)

- He is full of tenderness and mercy. (James 5:11)

- He keeps His word. (Isaiah 30:18)

- Those who come to Him for help will find great blessing. (Isaiah 30:18)

- He hears my anguish and cares about it. (Psalm 40:1 and Psalm 31:7)

- He acts in response to my cry for help and gives me new songs. (Psalm 40:2, 3)

- He has plans for me, and they are plans for my good. (Romans 8:28, Psalm 40:5)

- He will give strength and endurance. (2 Thessalonians 3:3)

- I can be confident that I will see His goodness. (Psalm 27:13, 14)

- I can pour out my heart to Him—there's no better place to go for help. (Psalm 62:1, 5-8)

- He is the great, almighty Creator, and He knows my troubles and will give me new strength and endurance beyond my own human limits. (Isaiah 40:26-31; Colossians 1:11)

- He is always working in me, towards the fulfillment of His plans. (Philippians 1:6)

- He says, "Don't be afraid or discouraged. I'm here to help you and give you strength." (Isaiah 41:10)

- I am one of His children and have a share in everything He's promised. (Colossians 1:11, 12)

Those verses all have personal meaning to me.

Look for His promises. If you're waiting in His presence, you'll find words meant especially for you in your time of waiting. They'll be words from Someone who loves you.

ANTHEM OF THOSE WHO WAIT

He has given me a new song to sing,
a hymn of praise to our God.
– from **PSALM 40:3** –

I grew up in a Mennonite church, singing the old hymns in four-part harmony without instrumental accompaniment. I loved singing and knew many of the hymns by memory, every word of every verse, even before I was a teenager.

"Come, Thou Fount of Every Blessing" was one of my favorites. I liked the tune and the poetic language.

Throughout the following decades, I learned the meaning of the words in that song—I lived them. And now, the hymn is still one of my favorites because it voices so much of my own journey. I've often thought that it could be called the "Pilgrim's Anthem."

We would be wise, I think, to make more of the Psalms a part of our worship. They are worship songs. Many were written by David, who was just as imperfect as I and yet had a special relationship with God. He wrote from the depths of his own experience—and many of his experiences are also ours. The Psalms have never become outdated.

Would someone please put more of the Psalms to music? Not just little snippets, but entire psalms, because often it is in the complete song that we find the deepest meanings.

Two good examples are Psalm 25 and Psalm 40. Both or either of these could be called the "Anthem of Those Who Wait."

Take a look at Psalm 25. We find these words in the opening verses:

O LORD, I give my life to you.
I trust in you, my God!

What wonderful sentiments! That's where we want to be while we wait, right? Standing solidly in our trust in God.

But take a closer look at the psalm. At this point, life is not rosy and wonderful for the songwriter. Look at verse 16: *I'm alone and in deep distress.* Verse 17: *My problems are going from bad to worse.* Verse 18: *Oh, LORD! Feel my pain, see my trouble, forgive all my sins!* Verse 19: *My enemies viciously hate me.* Verse 20: *Help! I need your protection!*

Do you hear the anguish? I would say this is a soul who is waiting for God to act.

Yet...

And here's where we can learn helpful things about how to wait. David's song would be a good pattern for us in our waiting.

First, we can tell that the writer of this song is in it for "the long haul." Things aren't looking good, but he is constantly and consciously, hour by hour, all day long, putting his hope in God. His opening lines set the tone: "I'm handing my whole life over to you." That, my friends, is confident hope.

Then, he makes a point of remembering all the things God has already done and all the times God has rescued him in the past.

And he constantly voices the goodness and love of God. He focuses on the Lord's faithfulness, His guidance, His mercy, His tender care of His people. (Just what we were doing in the previous meditation, as we listened to the voice of Someone who loves us.)

Psalm 40 follows the same pattern. This psalm adds a line I love: *He has given me a new song to sing, a new hymn of praise to our God.*

I think that's what happens to us when we wait in the ways outlined in Psalm 25 and Psalm 40. We put our lives in God's hands. We remember all the good things He has already done. We focus on His goodness and love toward us.

As a result, we learn new songs of praise! No matter how He answers our prayers, no matter when He answers, His goodness fills our waiting and our hope is strengthened and we learn even more of His high, deep, and wide love for us.

While we wait, we learn new songs.

And I have to smile. Because both psalms end exactly as we often end our prayers, with just a bit of prodding of our Father: *Please, hurry up and do something!*

꒰ꕤ "TRUST IN ME" ꕤ꒱

Let all that I am wait quietly before God, for my hope is in him. He alone is my rock and my salvation, my fortress where I will not be shaken.

– from PSALM 62:5-6 –

When you wait for something, you expect it, you know it's coming. Wait for God. Expect His help and rescue. *Know* that He keeps His word.

King David had many tough weeks; at times he was even so discouraged or frustrated that he *felt* as though God had forgotten him. But he always *knew* rescue would come. His hope was in one and only one Person, and this made his hope unshakeable.

Take a moment to read again the opening verses above...

Can you guess what word jumps out at me? Maybe it's the same word that smacked you.

Quietly.

Wait *quietly?*

I am much better at stewing and worrying and getting quite carried away with my own fretting.

But then I hear these words from King Jesus: *"Don't let your heart be troubled. Trust in God, and trust also in me"* (John 14:1).

There it is in a nutshell. That's hope: "Trust in me."

He says *Trust me* when the waiting has been long.

He says *Trust me* when our old nature rises up and pushes aside our best intentions.

He says *Trust me* when we are doubting, when we're discouraged, when we feel too weak for the battle.

He says *Trust me* when we're haunted by the past, fretting about the present, or worrying about the future.

"Don't let your heart be troubled," Jesus says to us. "Trust in God; and trust in me."

Ah! An *untroubled heart.* I want that!

Trusting Jesus is not a last resort or a life preserver we grab when we are desperate. Trusting Him is the *one* place where He wants us to live. Trusting Him is the *only* place where we can live fully the life He died to give us.

In this book, we're going to look at some of the many promises God has given us, bridges of hope to keep us moving forward. If we trust the Builder of the bridges of hope, then we can go forward in peace and confidence. We will not be shaken. We'll be living on that rock, in that fortress that the writers of Psalms recommend.

And if you do not yet trust Him, you might want to get to know Him. That's the only way to find out if it's safe to entrust your life and your hope to Him.

AND SO WE WAIT

Put your hope in the LORD. Travel steadily along His path.
- from **PSALM 37:34** -

And so we wait. The children of God live lives with heavenly dimensions, even while on this earth. And our earthly lives are built on waiting.

We wait for all that Jesus our Shepherd has promised for this earthly life. We wait for the strength to get through this day or the answer to a prayer tomorrow or a merciful miracle next week.

And we wait for much more. We wait for the grand culmination of all of God's plan—that plan for the rescue of the human race and a creation fresh and new. We wait for God's justice and the full inheritance promised the children of God. We wait to live in glorious realities yet to come.

But while we wait, we live in the *now*, and we're often perplexed, frustrated, saddened, or angered by the details of today and *now*.

We grow tired of planting seeds on barren ground. We all know the Biblical admonishment, "Do not be weary in well-doing." But sometimes, we do grow weary. Sometimes, we do want to give it up. Sometimes, we think all we do is in vain.

But when you cannot see the joy, when you grope in darkness for encouragement, when it seems you have nothing left within you to continue to plant hopeful seeds, then cling to the Vine for life and listen to the voice of Someone who loves you.

The Father says,

"Don't be afraid, for I am with you.
Don't be discouraged, for I am your God.
I will strengthen you and help you."
(Isaiah 41:10)

When we hold onto the Vine, the Vine holds us.

God has not left us to grope about blindly in the dark as we walk through this world. He has told us plainly who we are and who He is. He's told us His plan for creation and what He will do to help His children along their journey home to Him.

But still we wonder about the next step in this pilgrimage. What is ahead in the next hour? How will we get through this week? We are much concerned about the specifics of our own story within God's greater story.

That's where we're going in the following chapters. We'll look at many of the things we need to get through today, and we'll hear God's promise to supply what we need and His encouragement to *Trust me.*

And while you wait for the blossoming of His promise, fellow pilgrim, put your hope in Him and travel steadily along His path.

He does not forget us. He knows exactly what we need. Trust Him.

For more assurance for those who wait,
see the appendix for a list of additional Scriptures.

PRAYER TO HEAR THE HOPE:

Open my eyes to see the wonderful

truths in your instructions.

– **PSALM 119:18** –

HELP FOR OUR HOPE

BREATHED FOR OUR HOPE

Your word is my source of hope.

- from **PSALM 119:114** -

In our search for what is true and right, in our longing for God and our yearning to live as His children, how do we find our way?

All Scripture is inspired by God and is useful to teach us what is true and to make us realize what is wrong in our lives. It corrects us when we are wrong

*and teaches us to do what is right. God
uses it to prepare and equip his people to
do every good work.* (2 Timothy 3:16-17)

Some translations begin that passage saying,
"All Scripture is God-breathed..."

It's a good thing to read Scripture, even
memorize it. But the truth of Scripture sinks into
our bones and becomes part of us as we live out
the hope we find in God's Word.

I've always been fascinated by Chapter 119
of Psalms. Besides having the distinction of being
the longest chapter in the Bible, the psalm also
has the unique feature that every one of those
verses has a reference to God's Word—using
words like *commands, instruction, precepts.* The
psalmist sat down and wrote out a list, of sorts,
expressing everything the Word of God meant to
him.

The chapter is also right on target in showing
us how God's Word helps us live today.

For example, look at this practical verse:

*As pressure and stress bear down on
me, I find joy in your commands.* (Psalm
119:143)

Have you had any time recently when
pressure and stress bore down on you?

I've lived that verse. I know pressure and
stress bearing down on me and what those times

can do to me. And the best antidote I've found is the Word of God. It's the one thing that can get my life back in balance. It can repair the damage done to me by pressure and stress.

Scripture is life-giving and life-changing. It is a huge source of our hope. But the only way we discover the power of God's Word is when we try it for ourselves and make it our own by living it.

The composer of Psalm 119 also wrote "I will never forget your commandments, for by them you give me life" (verse 93). Our Father uses the guidance of Scripture to lead us to the life He wants to give us.

We often think the Bible is just a list of what we are to do and what we are not to do. It's true, God does show us the way He wants us to live. But Scriptures are much more than that—through the hope we find there, we also find the power, peace, and joy that He meant us to have when He first created us.

So it's worth taking a section here to reflect on what Psalm 119 promises us about the power of these words God has breathed for His children.

If you read through Psalm 119 and jot down everything the living Word will do, you'll have a long list. We don't have space here to look at 176 verses, so I'm going to pick out some of the hopes that over the last few decades have become part of my own bones.

⌒⌒⌒ FOR THOSE WHO LIE IN THE DUST ⌒⌒⌒

I lie in the dust; revive me by your word.

– **PSALM 119:25** –

Let's start at a personal level: Reflect on the days when you lie in the dust.

I know what this picture looks like in my own life: Flat. On my face. Feeling beat up. Grimy. Spent. Listless. Discouraged. With a ragged spirit. I've been there. And I expect that I'll be there again at times in the future.

I have often cried out this prayer as I go to my devotions: *I'm lying in the dust. Help! Revive me.*

And I can tell you, the Lord answers.

No matter if we are on the mountaintop with our head in the clouds and feel like we're flying or if we're lying face down with our nose in the dust and almost unable to breathe, the Spirit is there with us, and He'll use the living Word of God to enliven, encourage, comfort, and inspire us.

Hebrews 4:12 tells us the Word is alive and active, and 1 Thessalonians 2:13 assures us that it continually works in us. That's God's reality. It is a bridge of hope to keep us moving forward.

Even when we may feel quite the opposite, our hope knows the power of the Spirit and the Word is always at work in us. God never puts His plans "on hold" based on how we feel. He has adopted us as His children and given us the privileges and responsibilities of heirs; He's begun a work in us and He will finish it!

And to help our hope along the way, He has given us the Scriptures.

Sometimes all we can do is hold onto the promises that God never leaves us or abandons the work He is doing in us, always works for our good, and holds us in His love. Going to the words He has breathed for our benefit will reassure and revive us, like having a long, cold drink of water revives us when we are parched.

God's Word is given to us for many purposes. One of those purposes is to encourage, refresh, and comfort us when we desperately need it. It's the best place to go when we lie in the dust.

FINDING OUR HAPPINESS

Make me walk along the paths of your commands, for that is where my happiness is found.
– PSALM 119:35 –

Does the above title light a longing in your heart? Do you yearn to find the pathway to your own happiness? Wouldn't it be great to have a life full of joy?

The writer of Psalm 119 declares that the Word of the Lord lights the path to joy. He calls God's Word his greatest treasure. Wouldn't this also be considered a great treasure today—to have a formula or method or prescription for filling life with joy? Well, we've got it!

If we read the verses following verse 35, we can conclude that in the psalmist's day, people were looking for happiness in many of the same places people seek joy today: in the accumulation of money and possessions, in self-promotion, power, relationships, and all the same things our modern world promotes as keys to happiness.

But we will find our happiness just where the psalm writer did—in the paths of God's commands.

Even when our circumstances are not "happy," the joy in searching for and following the Lord flows through and grows in our lives. In verse 143, the psalmist says that when "pressure and stress bear down on me, I find joy in your commands." In another verse, the psalmist admits misery, but even then the joy he has found in God's word sustains him (see verse 92).

This declaration contrasts with the message of a world that says life must be rosy and filled with gratification for one to be happy. The message in Psalm 119 is, instead, that only the Word of God will feed and grow a joy that lives—even through misery and stress and hard times.

Can you identify with some of the psalmist's feelings? Ever feel pressure and stress suffocating you? Ever feel overcome with misery? Ever find yourself looking for the path to happiness?

Hope knows that in God's Word we do find the keys to our joy—even during the hardest times.

A SWORD FOR THE BATTLE

Guide my steps by your word,
so I will not be overcome by evil.
- PSALM 119:133 -

My oldest grandson was ten when he tried to teach me to play a Wii game. (Not an easy task, I can tell you.)

Holding the little white control, I tried to understand which button or movement would make me, the good guy on the screen, jump, twirl, kick, run, and transform into a super-hero, fighting the alien droids.

And then I discovered the secret. One push at the right time on the right button shot a shining, pulsating stream of light that looked like a sword (to my old-fashioned mind) straight toward the nasty creature advancing to attack me. I flicked my wrist and... aha! *Slice! Slice! Slice!* my lightsaber chopped up the menace and dispensed with that danger. On to the next alien! I sliced and chopped all advancing threats.

And in the middle of that Wii game, the Holy Spirit reminded me, "This is exactly what the Scriptures can do to all those things that attack you spiritually."

In Ephesians 6, Paul talks about strapping on all the armor God gives us against enemy attacks. Most of the items are armor, defenses against the enemy. But then Paul adds, "And take the sword of the Spirit, which is the word of God."

A sword is a weapon that can go on the offensive. The Spirit's weapon is the lightsaber of the Word of God. When I am under attack from things without and within, the Spirit uses the Word to slice up and dispatch those threats.

The Word fights our discouragement, our temptations, our doubt, our fears, our loneliness, our tendency toward envy and jealousy and anger and malice, our insecurities, our lack of faith, our blindness, our stubbornness, our bitterness, our hunger, our cynicism, our pride, our forgetfulness of God... I could go on and on.

I cannot explain to you *how* this all works

except to say that it is the mystery of the Spirit of Christ using the living Word of God within us. I can give you examples, though.

Take, for instance, the days when my past comes back to whisper accusations and remind me of my guilt. Then the Spirit steps in, brandishing the sword of all the promises and reassurances God has given to me, His beloved daughter, that the record against me has been canceled.

Or, when I slip into worrying about... well, I can worry about many things. But the Spirit reminds me of God's promise that my life is in His hands, and His love surrounds and holds me. Worry can be sliced up and discarded pretty quickly by the sword of the Word of God.

When I'm tempted to take the wrong path, whatever it might be, the Spirit uses God's words of guidance to steer me in the right direction. The sword slices up temptation.

Breathing His Word for us, God not only gave us an oasis of refreshment and a treasure that leads to joy, but also a weapon against all those things that would rob us of the life God has for His children.

∗∗∗ THE PLACE TO GO ∗∗∗
TO LEARN HOW TO LIVE

Your word is a lamp to guide my feet and a light for my path.
– PSALM 119:105 –

Where do you go for advice? When you've got a decision to make, choices to weigh, and action must be taken, who can you trust to steer you in the right direction? When you feel like you're groping in darkness for answers, where do you turn for a light?

Again and again, God's Word reminds us that His way of thinking is nothing at all like our human thinking and the principles and values of His Kingdom are quite different from the principles and values of this world. Thus, as children of the King, should we not be going to Him for our guidance and advice? Where in this world can we find better mentoring for living in God's Kingdom?

God's Word is given to light our way along a dark path. Its guidelines keep our focus on the right things, help us to see things as God sees them, and lead us to the life God has for us (verses 32, 37, 93 of Psalm 119). The apostle Paul explained that the Spirit uses the Word to show us God's thoughts (1 Corinthians 2:10-11).

Hear this advice from Isaiah:

*Look to God's instructions and teachings!
People who contradict his word are
completely in the dark.* (Isaiah 8:20)

All of this tells me that God wants us to
understand! He's not playing games with us. He
hasn't left us to figure things out on our own.
Instead, He has given us a treasure trove of
insight and wisdom and wise advice.

One of these verses that hits home for me is
verse 29 of Psalm 119:

*Keep me from lying to myself; give me the
privilege of knowing your instructions.*

How easy it is to lie to myself when I want
to justify or rationalize my actions! Sometimes I
do it consciously, attempting to convince myself.
Other times, the lies sneak in through my blind
spots or through unguarded doors and affect my
emotions and thinking.

Satan, the enemy of our souls, would love
to keep us living in the darkness of untruths,
deceived about our own worth, our relationships
to others, and our standing with God.

But the truth in God's Word shines light on
those deceptions and gives us the privilege of
knowing exactly what God has to say about those
matters.

God's Word is exactly that—His word to each

one of us. He's given us this precious gift, a light for the path we walk, as we strive to discern how to live.

⌒⌒⌒ TO WALK IN FREEDOM ⌒⌒⌒

I will walk in freedom, for I have devoted myself to your commandments.
– **PSALM 119:45** –

Walking in freedom. How I long for that!

In Galatians, the apostle Paul says that those who belong to Christ have been set free... to become slaves to God.

Does that seem a contradiction? And yet, in God's plan, that's the way it works. An utter and complete commitment to God's ways brings a freedom that can never be experienced outside of a devotion to God's truth. James wrote a letter about practical Christian living and said that God's Word is the "perfect law that sets you free" (James 1:25).

Want freedom? Look intently into the Word and do what it says! Again, to our human way of thinking this is a contradiction. A "law" brings freedom?

Again, *Yes.*

Jesus came to give us freedom. He says He is the truth, and that those who believe in Him will know the truth and the truth will set them free.

Those are familiar words. I wonder if you've experienced those words?

The more we soak our minds and hearts with Scripture and Jesus' words, the more we will understand that chains and prison bars once holding us have been broken and we are free.

Pursuing God's truth and devoting ourselves to it loosens the hold everything else has on us.

Those statements are so huge that I believe we will always be learning more of what He means; for all of our years, we'll be growing toward understanding this and growing out of our old lives and into the freedom He gives to His children.

Two things we can be sure of: Christ set us free so that we can live in freedom, and we will walk more and more in that freedom as we pour His Word into our hearts, minds, and souls.

I want it all. I'll say that boldly. Whatever God has for me, I want it all. I want freedom. And my hope knows it's there, in God's truth.

THE SECURITY OF "FOREVER"

*Those who love your instructions have great peace
and do not stumble.*

– PSALM 119:165 –

I have no idea where my life is going. When it will end. How it will end. What will come between now and the end. Who will be part of my remaining years. Who will not be here.

We can't see tomorrow. We can't control the future. But oh! We do try, don't we?

But even what we have and know today can change in the space of a few breaths.

We've all had the experience of depending on something that just... disappeared. It might have been something as simple as a favorite product you always used—until the manufacturer discontinued it. Or it might have been a person or a thing more vital to your life—a close friend, a job, or a bank account. You never expected to lose the friend or the job or the money; but one day, the thing you depended on was gone.

When we think we can depend on something or someone, we speak of standing on "solid ground." Yet even the most solid of earthly things will not last forever. Jesus said that even the earth and heavens will someday fade away—but His words will never fade away.

The psalmist reiterates throughout the entire Psalm 119: "Your word, O God, is eternal, standing firm in heaven. It will last forever and everything will serve your plans."

How good to know that God's truth will always stand! When we build our lives on the Scriptures, we are indeed putting our lives on the line—but we are trusting in truth and reality that will not change, will not disappear, will not become out-of-date or useless and ineffective.

We all put our security in *something.* It could be savings accounts, family, reputation, jobs, or the government. How about staking our lives on God's unchanging words of truth? Through all the tumult of life, God's truth will stand solid forever.

We may know nothing about what is ahead in our journey, but hope knows that we do not journey alone and God's words will always be a reliable, true guide for us.

When the foundation of our lives is the Word of God, we will not be disappointed, abandoned, or betrayed. We will know joy and wise counsel, hope, encouragement, and comfort. Anchored in the Word, we will have weapons against the enemy, tools to live fully, and light to keep on the right path.

God gave Isaiah a beautiful picture of how

His Word works:

> *"The rain and snow come down from the heavens and stay on the ground to water the earth. They cause the grain to grow, producing seed for the farmer and bread for the hungry. It is the same with my word. I send it out, and it always produces fruit. It will accomplish all I want it to, and it will prosper everywhere I send it."*
> (Isaiah 55:10-11)

My hope knows that God's Word is like life-giving water for the thirsty ground of my soul.

Why not saturate myself with all of its power?

For more on the power of God's Word,
see the appendix for a list of additional Scriptures.

PRAYER AS YOU TRUST GOD WITH YOUR LIFE:

O LORD, I give my life to you. I trust in you, my God!

– PSALM 25:1, 2 –

CARRIED IN HIS ARMS

Ე᳐ᲕᲘᲓᲛ MESSAGE OF HOPE ᲢᲕᲔᲕᲘᲒ

I made you and I will care for you.

- from ISAIAH 46:4 -

Life must have looked utterly bleak and hopeless. The country had been ravaged by a foreign king, crippled to the point that there seemed to be no hope the nation could ever rise again and come back to prosperity.

Babylon had smashed Israel. All of the leaders, the intelligentsia, the artisans, the brightest and best—anyone who could have been a spark of hope to the nation—were gone, deported to another country. The scattered and demoralized few that remained were governed by foreigners installed by Babylon.

Then God sent the prophet Isaiah to those still left in Israel. His message was to comfort and reassure them:

> *"Listen to me, descendants of Jacob, all you who remain in Israel. I have cared for you since you were born. Yes, I carried you before you were born. I will be your God throughout your lifetime—Until your hair is white with age. I made you, and I will care for you. I will carry you along and save you."* (Isaiah 46:3-4)

They may have been asking where God was when the Babylonians were destroying their country. (We tend to do that, too, don't we?) But God assured them—He was still carrying them. They were going through troubled times, but that did not mean God had abandoned them.

These verses are bookended by passages that ridicule the idols of the Babylon culture. Those idols were made by craftsman and were carried around and worshipped, but were deaf and dumb, could not move, and "when someone prays to it, there is no answer. It can't rescue anyone from trouble" (verse 7).

In contrast, God reminded the Israelites just who their God was. He reminded them of His constant care. His rescue. His help. His provision. He did not need to be carried around. *He* was carrying *them.*

The God who was speaking these lines is not a God of the past. He is the God of our today. These words are spoken to every child of God.

The God who never changes cared for you already before the time you began your walk on this earth (stop a moment and think about that) and will continue to care for you until the end of your walk. He carries you along—and how many times we all need to be carried!

Our God is not detached, uncaring, and arbitrary. We are constantly, unfailingly in His loving care. Compare the unreliability of the idols the world hopes in: financial "security"; personal resources, relationships; power; or social standing.

This hope that the Creator God watches over and acts on behalf of His people changes everything. We can move forward with certainty that at every step of our way, our God will provide what we need.

He will carry us.

⤳⤳ GUARDING OUR SOULS ⤳⤳

Once you were like sheep who wandered away. But now you have turned to your Shepherd, the Guardian of your souls.
– 1 PETER 2:25 –

Why do so many people hold tightly to Psalm 23? Why is that passage so often read when there's a need for comfort?

Because it answers the cries of our hearts— for every one of us, at so many different places in our lives. At our darkest moments, when we are most fearful, when we long for rest, when we are hungry and thirsty, when we are too exhausted to go on, when we feel lost, when we face devastating foes.

The words of Psalm 23 respond to those needs in us that require Someone bigger than us, stronger than us. Our Shepherd has resources far beyond our own.

Before he was a warrior and king, David was a shepherd. He understood the heart of a good shepherd who supplies everything his flock needs, from food and water to protection against the fiercest of predators. In the picture of the shepherd caring for his sheep, David saw himself as the one in need and looked to God to provide for and watch over him. "The LORD is my shepherd," he declared. "I have all that I need."

Most of us know nothing about sheep, but we all do know about the human needs listed in Psalm 23. And David declared that God meets all those needs. Souls who need comfort and protection can go to the Shepherd.

The theme of God shepherding His flock, caring for and providing what His people need, is carried throughout the entire Bible. This is one of the best reasons to read the Old Testament—to follow the history of God's persistent care for His people.

God created, and then His creation turned away from Him. But He did not leave it alone to whirl along to its doom. He actually came to earth in the person of the Great Shepherd, Jesus Christ. He came to gather the wandering and lost sheep, to provide for their needs, and to love them deeply. And in the end, He died a human death so that His flock could gain immortality.

Everything that David knew of God's shepherd love (outlined in Psalm 23) is found in Jesus:

He gives us that longed-for rest and food and water that satisfy fully.

He provides His strength and guidance and is always close, protecting and comforting us in even the darkest times.

He has beaten all our enemies.

This is what the Great Shepherd provides for all who come to Him. He is the guardian of our souls' well-being.

✤ "DO NOT WORRY" ✤

He will certainly care for you.
Why do you have so little faith?
- MATTHEW 6:30 -

The birds are very busy at the time I write this. On early morning walks, I find myself stopping frequently to peer into the just-greening trees, trying to find the source of any song I cannot recognize. They're advertising for mates and building nests—nests made of twigs and strings and straw that, amazingly, will withstand the onslaught of strong storms. And other birds are still traveling through, on the way to their summer homes. Migration is, to my mind, one of the great wonders of God's creation.

I'm reminded of Jesus' words to look at the birds, who don't plant or harvest or store food because God feeds them. And we are more valuable to Him than the birds. Jesus pointed to the lilies in their splendor, here today and gone tomorrow. If God cares for them, why can't we believe that God will care for those He calls His children?

That is who we are to God. He calls us His children (1 John 3:1). His care and provision for us go beyond anything we know in our human relationships. The psalmist wrote that "even if my father and mother abandon me, the LORD will hold me close" (Psalm 27:10).

That is the picture of our Shepherd, holding us close, knowing exactly what we need. Jesus noted that unbelievers' thoughts are constantly taken up with worries about food, drink, and clothing, but those who believe God do not need to worry—God knows exactly what we need. "He will certainly care for you. Why do you have so little faith?" asked Jesus.

Jesus is speaking that question to me. His question shoots some pain through my heart.

His words aren't condemning, scolding words. They are tender. He is encouraging me to relax and trust Him.

I want to believe. I want to live fully assured of God's care. I want to live on Jesus' promise that we don't have to worry about tomorrow. But I have not yet achieved a worry-free faith. I guess my faith is still "little."

Psalm 106 recounts the history of the children of Israel and describes what happened when they finally reached the borders of the Promised Land: "The people refused to enter the pleasant land, for they wouldn't believe his promise to care for them" (verse 24).

That's one of the saddest lines in the Bible. There they were. On the threshold of all the wonderful things God had promised them. They could have had the life they'd been seeking for forty years. Yet they did not move forward because they didn't believe that God would keep His promises and take care of them.

Dear Jesus, I don't want that to describe my life.

If God has wonderful things for me, I don't want to miss out because I don't believe His promises.

We can have faith in God's care for us. We're far more valuable to Him than the birds and the lilies. Think about what He has done to bring us into His family.

Spirit, help my unbelief. Grow my faith!

CONSTANTLY WATCHING OVER US

Praise the Lord; for each day he carries us in His arms.
- from PSALM 68:19 -

My friend Sue was out on the highway, driving home late at night during one of the worst snow and ice storms we had that winter. The route home went around curves and up and down hills. Road crews were out, but the roads were icing over and the snow came down so fast that highways once plowed were soon covered again.

She gripped the wheel and peered through the driving snow, praying, asking God to get her home safely.

Then, as she approached the intersection where she would turn left, out of the blowing snow on her right appeared a snowplow. It passed in front of her, proceeding down the road toward her home, going ahead of her and plowing the way, right up to the little country road leading to her house.

She says it was just like a reassuring embrace from her Father, telling her He was there, taking care of her.

A "lucky coincidence"? Just a matter of "good timing"? That's what many might say.

But we who hold this great hope—that our God watches over us—would agree with my friend's view of the situation: The Lord was watching over her, taking care of her. Constantly.

> "The LORD himself watches over you! The one who watches over you never sleeps, but watches over your life as you come and go." (see Psalm 121)

The above lines come from Psalm 121, a short psalm of just eight verses. Yet in those eight verses, the writer repeats five times that the Lord watches over us, "both now and forever."

This is what our hope knows: Our lives are in His hands. He provides for us, does not forget us, and never abandons us. He is not a distant God. He's with us every moment, carrying us, holding us, and helping us.

～⁓᠈⁓ THAT DIVINE POWER ⁓᠈⁓᠈

*By His divine power, God has given us everything
we need for living a godly life.*

– 2 PETER 1:3 –

"I trust in the Lord... "

"Your times are in my hands."

"Cast all your cares on the LORD, for He careth for you."

When life is rolling merrily along, when life is good, then those words from Scripture come easily to our lips. But when we've been without a job for two years, or when the bad guys seem to be winning, or when we're not sure how we'll pay the rent that was due last week, or when we unexpectedly hear a grim diagnosis, or when we lie awake at night worrying about the daughter who has left home, then the words are much more difficult to say... and even more difficult to live.

What we can hold onto is a phrase from the opening verse: *By his divine power.*

We're going back to that verse we started with. Focus on the divine power. In every promise we will look at in these pages, we depend on divine power. That is the only reason we have this hope. If all depends on our own strength, resources, and power, then we're sunk. But it is His divine power that cares for us, protects us, and provides for us.

This is the bolster for my "little" faith. My faith reads the promises, mentally says, *I believe,* but may still struggle to trust God's care. I must rest, finally, in trusting His divine power that makes all things possible.

With that power in focus, we can pray— regardless of our circumstances—the Psalm prayer for this section: "O LORD, I give my life to you. I trust in you!"

Our hope rests on a divine power.

SO, IF GOD IS FOR US...

This I know: God is on my side!
I praise God for what He has promised.
– **PSALM 56:9-10** –

We've just spent more than a few pages focusing on the promise that God cares for and watches over His people. That "caring for" covers many details, many needs, many different seasons of our lives. From this general reminder of that promise, we'll go into some of the specific needs we have: the need for wisdom, strength, encouragement, refreshment, and security, to name a few.

But here are just a few more reminders that our hope can trust in our Shepherd's care:

Give your burdens to the LORD, and he will take care of you. (Psalm 55:22)

And we know that God causes everything to work together for the good of those who love God and are called according to His purpose for them. (Romans 8:28)

What shall we say about such wonderful things as these? If God is for us, who can ever be against us? Since he did not spare even his own Son but gave him up for us all, won't he also give us everything else? (Romans 8:31-32)

These words are God's reality. Are we going to trust these promises?

Once we start focusing on His reality, our lives change. Psalm 112 has a few lines that light a longing in my heart: "They do not fear bad news; they confidently trust the Lord to care for them. They are confident and fearless..." (verses 7, 8).

Confident and fearless. I want to live that way!

God is for me. God is for you. We can trust Him to care for us.

For more promises of God's care,
see the appendix for a list of additional Scriptures.

PRAYER TO ASK FOR GOD'S HELP:

I need help.

– **PSALM 86:1** –

"I'M HERE TO HELP YOU"

THE ONE WHO WILL HELP ME

For I hold you by your right hand—I, the LORD your God.
And I say to you, 'Don't be afraid. I am here to help you'.

– ISAIAH 41:13 –

Sometimes when I'm close to the edge of despair, I look around at the natural world.

If it's possible, I like to sit by the sea and watch the endless cycle of tides. Or stroll through tall, fragrant firs. Admire an eagle or hawk, and wonder what it's like to drift high above the earth. Marvel at the delicate details of a beautiful flower. Go out at night and be dazzled by the number of stars.

And I look at my body: how fingers, eyes, muscles, and organs are intricately woven to work as one. Or I watch my grandchildren with delight and amazement at the miracle of family.

Soaking up the beauty and wonders of God's creation reminds me: *My God has done all this. Surely He can handle my current predicament.*

I often feel as though I'm just not enough. There is not enough in me to run the race today, to fight the good fight, to be all that I must be.

Sometimes, that's how I feel. And in one sense, my feelings are accurate. I am not "enough." But God's promise is that I do not face anything alone. He says, *Don't be discouraged. Don't be afraid. I am here to help you.*

This is His promise: I do not have to live on my own resources, will, and strength. My Father is going to help me through today. His Word says that He is *always* ready to help us (Psalm 46:1).

Think of a time when you were overwhelmed by a project or a chore. Then a friend showed up and said, "I'm here to help you." Have you known the relief that comes?

Know also that the almighty God who created this universe shows up every day and says, "I'm here to help you."

The psalmist was thinking of this amazing promise when he wrote, "Because you are my helper, I sing for joy in the shadow of your wings. I cling to you; your strong right hand holds me securely"(Psalm 63:7-8).

Ah, yes! Doesn't it change everything to know that the God who spoke the glories of nature into existence has also promised that He is always right here to help us? To help *you* and *me.*

Focus on the Lord's greatness. We can have confidence and hope. We can be strong and courageous. Because it doesn't all depend on us. We are not enough. But we are surrounded and covered and supported by the greatness of a God who loves us deeply, a God who is on our side and is here to help.

～✦✦↣ ON THE PATH WITH US ↢✦✦～

But for those who are righteous, the way is not steep and rough. You are a God who does what is right, and you smooth out the path ahead of them.

– ISAIAH 26:7 –

One Monday morning, I looked at my calendar and felt the beginnings of panic stir within.

There's no way I can do all this, I thought.

As I considered what still must be done on several projects, meeting the deadlines looked impossible. And there was more than business deadlines on my calendar that week—several family and personal commitments must be honored. Each item was something I considered a "must-do." I could not postpone any of it until the next week. (I'm a good procrastinator. Have had lots of practice.)

I need help, Lord! That was about all I could pray that Monday morning.

Then I decided there was nothing else to do but jump into the week.

By Thursday noon, everything was done.

At the beginning of the week, I had thought the ship was going to sink under me. I had scheduled far too much to keep all my promises. But instead, the ship sailed into harbor and dropped anchor two days early.

How did that happen?

Honestly, I was astonished.

Then I "stumbled" across the verse from Isaiah that is quoted at the beginning of this meditation. I believe that God uses His Word to speak to us and many times shows us passages we need at the very time we need to learn something. At the end of that miraculous week, God showed me that verse and said, *That's what I did for you this week.*

I can be pretty good at complaining, whining, and feeling sorry for myself. It's not pretty, and not what I want to be. But there is some sort of default setting in me that kicks me into that mode of thinking.

I want to change that setting. So I'm asking the Holy Spirit to teach me to see my life from the perspective of this Isaiah verse. The promise might sound too good to be true, but as I watch for God's help in my journey, I see that He does smooth out my path. Focusing on God's help in my life goes a long way in eliminating whining and feeling sorry for myself.

Please don't think that I subscribe to the current American attitude that a "good" life should be easy and conflict-free. That's just not true. I know this earthly life will always have its troubles and hard times. And often, we ourselves are responsible for the predicaments in which we find ourselves.

God doesn't shield us from the difficult paths. (In another section, we'll meditate on His promises for good things coming out of hard places.) But He does help us through everything.

I believe that no matter what you are facing today or why you are in the spot you're in, God is ready to help you. And if you ask for His help,

He can smooth the bumps a bit for you.

It's not complaining or whining or feeling sorry for ourselves when we look to our heavenly Father and say, *Can you smooth out this path, Father? I need help getting through this.*

✤✤ IN DARK VALLEYS, TAKE HEART ✤✤

Let all who are helpless take heart. Come, let us tell of the
LORD's greatness... Those who look to him
for help will be radiant with joy.
– from PSALM 34:2, 3, 5 –

My over-scheduled week may seem like a small "trouble" to you. As I write, my mind constantly goes back to the news this week: another school shooting. Children dead. Parents grieving. My stewing over a heavy work load seems silly in comparison.

Yet "real life" is made up of both the simple struggles of getting through our day and the walks we must make through the darkest valleys imaginable. We all know times that we are caught in circumstances that shake and threaten to break our lives, and we feel so helpless.

But *real life,* for those who are living in God's kingdom, is that no matter what our circumstances, we are never help-less.

Psalm 34 was written by a man who lived through a great deal of trouble: Family turmoil. A much-loved but rebellious son trying to kill him (try to imagine *that* dark valley). Betrayal by people he trusted. Powerful and deceitful people working against him. A heavy burden of guilt because of wrong choices. And even feelings of estrangement from the God he loved and depended on.

Psalm 34 is a life we can identify with. There are feelings of helplessness, desperation, trouble, and fear—things we face every day. We find ourselves helpless in the face of a diagnosis or the conflicts in a relationship. Finances that don't stretch far enough create anxiety. We walk in a world filled with monstrous evil. We are not immune to all that brings pain and tears.

Psalm 34 is real life, with real-life troubles. But yet, look what the writer declares:

> *I will praise the LORD at all times. I will constantly speak his praises. I will boast only in the LORD; let all who are helpless take heart. I prayed to the LORD, and he answered me. He freed me from all my fears.* (Psalm 34:1-2, 4)

Side by side with trouble and turmoil, we also find joy and praise and gladness. Freedom from fear. Exuberance, even!

That's the life I want! But how do I get that? The psalm tells us:

Those who look to him for help will be radiant with joy... Taste and see that the LORD *is good. Oh, the joys of those who take refuge in him!* (verses 5, 8)

When we feel helpless, we can take heart because we are not without help. We can take heart because the Lord's eyes and ears are open to His people and He is good. He will answer!

In the songs he wrote, David teaches us these things:

- Constantly praise the Lord.

- Remember who the Lord is and what He has done.

- Remember that He comes to rescue us and will also bless us with good things even in the midst of trouble.

I'm beginning to see that when we *tell of the Lord's goodness* and *speak of the greatness of our Father,* we are administering an antidote for the feeling of helplessness. It's one of the ways we can *take heart.*

In the face of all the trouble in David's life, he knew a joy and security that arose from this fact: "Even though I walk through the darkest valley, I will fear no evil, for you are with me."

I'm not going to leave you alone, Jesus says to us.

It may be only ripples of small troubles upsetting our day. Or it could be a terrifying tidal wave sweeping over our life and threatening to drown us. No matter what, our Father hears his people when they call to him for help (Psalm 34:17).

Lord, I need help!

That prayer is always heard, and the helpless are never without help.

WHERE'S THE JOY?

Because you are my Helper,
I sing for joy in the shadow of your wings.
– PSALM 63:7 –

Pause for just a moment and answer a question: When you feel helpless and overwhelmed, where do you go?

We in Western culture are programmed to be self-reliant, strong, assertive, empowered. We know all the buzz words that today's self-help mentality promotes.

But what does God say?

Those who look to him for help will be radiant with joy. (Psalm 34:5)

Oh, the joys of those who take refuge in [the Lord]! (Psalm 34:8)

But joyful are those who have the God of Israel as their helper, whose hope is in the Lord their God. (Psalm 146:5)

When we try to be so self-sufficient, do we miss the joy that bubbles through the trouble of Psalm 34?

Those who look to Him for help and those who take refuge in Him are the ones who find radiant joy. Note that in every case, the writer still needs help and refuge. There's still trouble and sorrow in life, but joy is the focus, not the trouble. I'll take that any day—trading my despair for radiant joy!

Are we looking to the wrong places for our help? Is that why we do not find joy in the midst of our troubles? Is that why all seems so dark, hopeless, and helpless? The Word warns us not to look to the wrong things for help—powerful people, money, or, yes, even our own strength. All of those fail us. God never does.

Many years ago, the Medical Mission Sisters recorded a song called "Joy is like the Rain." The lyrics talk about finding joy in the middle of trouble and storms. This line from the song came back to me today: *Christ asleep within my boat, whipped by wind yet still afloat...*

That's us! Our boat can be whipped by the elements but still floating, because, as another old hymn says, *Nothing can swallow the ship where lies, the Master of ocean and earth and skies!*

Well, now I've got songs going round in my head.

Where is this joy in the midst of trouble? It is that we have the God who holds the universe in His hands as our helper

We may even need His help to see His help and find this joy. If so, I believe God will also answer the prayer, *Lord, I need help in seeing and knowing how great and mighty your help is.*

⊱⊰⊱⊰ CHARIOTS OF FIRE ⊱⊰⊱⊰

Let all who are helpless take heart. Come, let us tell of the LORD's greatness... Those who look to him for help will be radiant with joy.
- from PSALM 34:2, 3, 5 -

Let's imagine what that morning must have been like.

Elisha and his servant woke up one morning in a small town in the hill country of Samaria. The servant, out on an early morning errand, was stunned by the sight of chariots and foot soldiers in positions around the town. The enemy had moved into place under the cover of darkness. These were the troops of Aram, who had been raiding towns in Samaria, trying to break the country bit by bit. They were after Elisha.

The servant was afraid. The enemy forces were formidable, they were everywhere, and there was no apparent way of escape. They were probably doomed to be captured or killed. He ran back home to report the situation to Elisha.

"What will we do?" the servant asked.

Elisha was not afraid. "We have more on our side!" he declared.

I'm sure the young servant was puzzled at such an answer.

Then Elisha prayed. He did not ask God to come and rescue them. No, instead he prayed for his young servant. He asked God to open the young man's eyes to see the truth of their situation. "Let him see!" Elisha requested.

The Lord opened the young man's eyes, and when he looked up, he saw that the hillside around Elisha was filled with horses and chariots of fire. (2 Kings 6:17)

Elisha knew something that the young servant still had to learn. Perhaps it's something we also need to learn.

Oh, Lord, open our eyes and let us see. Let us see Your constant presence to help us.

Yes, this story is from the Old Testament, but God says He does not change. Scripture tells us what is still true today: the eyes of the Lord are constantly on those who rely on His love, His ears are always open to our prayers, and He's always ready to help. He is there, constantly, without fail.

Let us see the power with which you protect us and provide for us.

Chariots of fire? Who knows? Are there angels fighting for us in the spiritual realm? We have Scriptures that would indicate this is happening. But God also sends his "angels" in human form, people sent into our lives at just the right time for the purpose of strengthening, encouraging, teaching, and supporting us. They are—just like heavenly angels—special representatives sent by God for a certain purpose.

We need not despair, even when the situation looks grim to our blind eyes. We need not feel helpless or hopeless when faced with situations we think are impossible. Jesus said, "Do not be afraid of any trouble you face in the world. Trust God. Trust me."

What would this day look like if we could clearly see the chariots of fire surrounding us? What if we could have a taste—just one wee sip— of the might of God's incredible, divine power at work in our lives?

❧ SENT TO TAKE CARE OF US ❧

*Angels are only servants—spirits sent to care for people
who will inherit salvation.*
- **HEBREWS 1:14** -

We were on a two-lane highway winding through the woods in the spectacular New Hampshire White Mountains.

My friend Betty was driving when the rain started, just a light spattering of droplets. I was reading a map when suddenly the windshield gave a loud *crack!* We'd been slapped by something neither one of us saw coming. I jumped and wondered what had hit us.

Rain, it turned out—a sheet of rain, driven by wind so strong that Betty soon said, "I can't control the car!" She wrangled with the steering wheel, and managed to get the car off the road, into the parking area in front of a building that looked like an auto repair shop. There was no one around except a woman in a red car who had also pulled over.

The rain came in torrents and the wind howled and tore at the trees around us. I watched the power lines whip back and forth and wondered if there was any safe place for us to be.

The fury lasted only five minutes. Then the wind lessened, but the rain kept up, steadily pounding the car.

The red car pulled back onto the road, and in a moment, we, too, cautiously started out. Leaves had been stripped from trees, and small branches were scattered everywhere. We could easily avoid most of the debris, but water was now flooding the road at places. Along one stretch, a muddy torrent came tumbling down the mountainside, rushing over the highway. Was it safe for us to continue?

There was nowhere to stop, nowhere to find refuge. The strong currents flooding over the road looked deep and dangerous. And if we met a vehicle coming the other way, was there room to pass? If we did stop, might we be caught and even washed away by a flash flood? If we drove through that water, might we be driving into a hole where the road had caved in?

We had no choice but to continue on. So we did. Carefully. With an *Oh, Lord, help us!*

I looked back. A white pickup was following us. I hadn't noticed it when we pulled out of the parking area. The red car ahead of us had turned down a side road almost immediately, and for a while, there had been no other traffic on the road. But now I kept an eye on that white pickup that had appeared. It was comforting to know someone else was there, in case we did end up in the ditch, or worse.

Neither of us remembers how long it took to travel that lonely stretch of highway in the rain, with torrents washing over the pavement, carrying debris and gouging out holes. But, happily, the white truck stayed with us.

At last, we came to a small town, stopped at the first eatery we saw, and breathed a sigh of relief. The rain slowed to a drizzle and the sun even came from behind the clouds as we walked into the restaurant.

The white pickup was gone.

"He was our angel escort," said Betty with conviction.

As far as I know, during my formative years in church, no sermon was ever preached about angels. I was in church two or three times a week and never heard a discussion on these beings. As a result, I must admit that I never gave much thought to them. Yes, angels are mentioned at numerous places in the Bible—they even play important roles in several accounts—but somehow, nothing had reached my head or heart to prompt me to look for angel help in my own journey. I can't explain it exactly, but perhaps I felt that angels were only a part of life "back then" and not something I could count on today.

That evening in the White Mountains sent me on a search of Scriptures. I wanted to know what God had to tell us about angels.

And here are some of the things I found:

- The angel of the LORD guards, surrounds, and defends those who fear God. (from Psalm 34:7)

- His angels are ordered to protect those who live in the shelter of the Most High. (from Psalm 91:11)

- When Daniel was thrown to the lions, it was an angel who came to shut the lions' mouth. (from Daniel 6:22)

- Angels were messengers from God to Mary and the shepherds. (from Luke 1:26 and 2:9)

- On the morning of Jesus' resurrection, an angel rolled the stone away from the tomb (from Matthew 28:2), and the guards knew this was no ordinary being. They shook with fear and fainted.

- When Peter was thrown into prison, an angel came in the night and freed him. (from Acts 12:7)

- After forty days of fasting and trials in the wilderness, when the devil finally left Jesus alone (can you imagine how exhausted He must have been?), angels came to take care of Him. (from Matthew 4:11)

- During Jesus' struggle in Gethsemane—while His human nature was in agony because He knew what was ahead and His humanity wanted to avoid it—an angel came from heaven and strengthened Him. (from Luke 22:43)

There's more about angels, but these are references that spoke to me. Hebrews 1:14 sums it up: Angels are sent to care for God's children.

Now, I am counting on that. I'm looking for it!

As we ate supper that night, Betty and I talked about our trip through the storm. We agreed: in spite of the furor of the elements, we had both felt securely wrapped in God's care.

ᰔᰆᰅ COMMIT AND TRUST ᰆᰕᰖᰅ

Commit everything you do to the LORD.
Trust him, and he will help you.
- PSALM 37:5 -

On one of the days I worked on this section, another item on my schedule was to fulfill a promise. That item staring at me from my calendar was troubling me.

The problem was that keeping my promise would, I suspected, upset the person with whom I had made a pact.

You see, I had promised to review a book and then publish that review. But when I read the novel, I found that I could not give it a high rating or even recommend it, due to the way the author had handled the subject matter. The perspective that was presented, I felt, was neither true nor uplifting. I feared the book would harm more than heal.

But I had to publish that review for two reasons: I had promised to do it, and I could not back down from writing what I felt was truth.

When I pushed the "Publish" button and sent the review off into Amazon World, I did so with a prayer: *Okay, I've done it, Lord. It's up to You what You want to do with it.*

I had to let the whole thing in God's hands. But it was hard to do that. What if there were angry or bitter repercussions? What if my online review triggered a slew of hate mail? What if... ?

Yet, there was nothing I could do to control the outcome. I had written what I felt led to write—I had prayed about this for weeks, when I saw the pickle I was in. I had begged the Spirit for guidance in my thinking, in my choice of words, and in my attitude as I wrote. I wanted to commit the entire process to the Lord. And so, as I hit that last button, everything was in His hands.

But I don't want you to think it was easy to publish those written words. It was very, very hard.

Commit and trust. Those are two big words. They demand a lot of us. They ask everything of us. But, as in so many other things, the Spirit will help us if we ask. And that was my prayer: Help me to let go of anxiety over this. *Help me to let You take care of results and consequences.*

Take a moment to re-read the opening verse. Note the challenge and the promise.

How simple are those instructions? Commit everything today to the Lord. And trust Him.

The promise that follows: He will help you.

Our lessons here are straight from the Bible and the dictionary.

What do you do when you *commit?* One meaning is to give something in trust, or to entrust for safekeeping. That reminds me of a verse I hang onto... *My times are in your hands,* LORD (see Psalm 31:15). If we can say that, honestly and fervently, then we have committed our lives to His safekeeping.

A second meaning is to *bind or pledge*

oneself to. When I'm committed to some person or principle or purpose, that commitment shapes my thoughts and behavior. When I'm committed to the Lord—pledged and bound to Him—then whatever I do, I'm doing for Him (Ephesians 6:7 and Colossians 3:23).

I'm going to take a moment here—and encourage you to do so, too—to think about what I've planned for this day. Everything. Even the little, mundane, insignificant details. Have I committed everything to Him?

Put it all in His hands. Entrust it to Him. Rely on Him. Pledge this day to Him.

Committing and trusting does require every bit of me. But there's the promise: He will help me!

He doesn't promise that it will be easy. He doesn't promise that I will always have the results I want. But He promises He is there, in every moment, to help me. He delights in every detail of my life, He directs my steps, and though I do stumble, I will never fall, because the Lord holds my hand (Psalm 37:23-24).

I'm still working at my part—the committing and trusting part. My hope is counting on His help and His holding me.

⸺ HELP IN OUR WEAKNESS ⸺

And the Holy Spirit helps us in our weakness.
– from ROMANS 8:26 –

I wanted to scream at him. Screaming would have vented my frustration. I wanted even more than a scream. I also wanted to let loose all the sharp and nasty things clamoring to get out of my head and let them fly right at him. Then I'd stomp away. Maybe slam a door, for good measure. The man was just so difficult, so bullheaded, so negative.

I didn't let fly with my own ammunition. Or do any of the other things I wanted to do. I do think God must have intervened and guarded my tongue.

But Jesus and I... well, for a long time after that, we were still having a conversation about my attitude and feelings that evening.

We might think that it would have been wonderful to live when Jesus did, to be able to walk along with Him, listening to His teaching, learning from Him. To follow Him when He lived as a man on this earth.

But that might be only a wistful imagining.

The truth might be that we probably would

have been just like the twelve disciples He did choose. Many times unable to understand. Slow to grasp what He was trying to show us. Frequently arguing amongst ourselves. At times, totally missing His point. There were some who followed Him but then decided to give it up—His teaching was just too hard.

Yes, I think Jesus was probably often frustrated with the lack of understanding He saw in His disciples.

But here's what is amazing to me: Not only do I get to walk with Jesus on my pilgrimage through this life, now, in this time, but He accepted me as His disciple in spite of what and who I was. And He's helping me to become who and what God intends His children to be.

Jesus left His disciples on earth, but He promised them a Helper. The same promise is made to us, to everyone who believes. He doesn't leave us alone to sink or swim on our own. The same Helper sent to Jesus' first disciples—the Holy Spirit—is sent to us, to live with us, to help and teach and guide.

My hope is depending on that. I've staked my life on the help of the Helper.

The opening verse for this meditation is taken from a sequence of three chapters in Romans that spend a great deal of time talking about the constant struggle between the old me, selfish and stubborn, and the "new me," created to be a child of God. *Every day* these two natures fight for control. I could have written those chapters, because I know that battle. It's a constant in my life.

But even in the struggle, God always works for our good, is always for us, and will never withdraw His love. And someday the battle will be done. We will be perfect in every way, even with new bodies!

Someday.

But what about in the meantime? Left to rely on my own resources, I would lose the battle. Old habits and thinking and impulses have a strong grip on me.

God's plan is to help us in this battle. The Holy Spirit, our Helper, never leaves us. He is always there to guide and teach and form in us a new character, one befitting a child of God.

We don't have to do it ourselves. It doesn't all depend on us. That's good news, because the weakness in me is probably my worst enemy. I need much help in my weakness. Philippians 2:13 says that God is working in us, changing our hearts and our characters to be what pleases Him. That's something I could never do on my own.

God's Spirit is creating a new me! That's true help and rescue.

My weakness is not only in dealing with the old me. I also need much help in making wise choices, in fighting discouragement, in finding strength and comfort, in seeking solutions. When we call for help, His Spirit is there to guide and teach and strengthen.

I sit down to write sometimes with a mind that refuses to open up and be creative. *Lord, I need help.*

I've driven through crazy, life-threatening traffic with no idea what turn was coming next. *Lord, I need help.*

I've had to navigate a stressful, busy day with three hours of sleep. *Lord, I need help.*

I've dreaded having to deal with a difficult person. *Lord, I need help.*

I've held onto grudges, unwilling to give them up. *Lord, I need help.*

I've been just like some of those disciples— thinking that Jesus' way is just too hard, and wanting to do things my own way and not His. *Lord, I really need help!*

Jesus the Rescuer has come to live with me. It's even better than living when He was on earth. Now He never walks away from me to go up into the hills to pray by Himself, or leaves me alone while He's off on some other mission. We are walking together. He is teaching me as we go along. Guiding me. Helping me. Forming His character in me... even though I'm a slow learner. By His Spirit, He's helping me along the journey through this life to another more perfect life.

Amazing. My hope is counting on it.

TEARING OPEN, BURSTING THROUGH!

So be strong and courageous, all you who put your hope in the LORD!

– PSALM 31:24 –

Let's look at a few more Old Testament stories, because I like these so much and because they hold truths for us...

After David had finally been anointed king, the Philistines soon marched against him. Their army was spread out in the valley in front of David's fortress, and David went to God for advice.

"Should I go and fight them? Will you hand them over to me?" David asked.

"Yes," God replied. "Go. I will certainly do it."

So David went out to battle and smashed the enemy.

But he took no credit himself. The credit all went to the Lord. "The Lord burst through my enemies like a raging flood!" said David, and he named the place Baal-perazim, which means *the Lord who bursts through.*

Wouldn't you like to have the Lord burst through your enemies?

Psalm 18 paints a great picture of God tearing open the heavens and coming down Himself to rescue one who depended on His help. Wouldn't it be great if God tore open the heavens and came to your rescue in impossible situations?

He does.

He has torn open heaven and come down not only to rescue us, but to live with us. He comes to abide with His children. He makes His home with us and shares life with us.

Do we see God bursting through to help us? He does it every day, in ways huge and small. Do we ask for our eyes to be opened to see it?

Story Two:

The Philistines, bullies that they were, did not give up. They took some time to recover, then came back another day.

Again David went to God for help. This time, God gave him a strategy for the battle: Circle around behind. Attack them near the poplar trees. And "when you hear a sound like marching feet in the tops of the poplar trees, be on the alert! That will be the signal that the Lord is moving ahead of you to strike down the Philistine army." (The story is in 2 Samuel 5.)

The sound of marching feet in the tops of the poplar trees. That image fascinates me. Like the chariots of fire that Elijah saw coming to their rescue, God sent a squad to rescue David.

My hope knows that God is still the same God, rescuing and helping His children. He says to us today, "I am here to help you." I've heard the wind move the autumn leaves of poplar trees. It reminds me that the Lord moves ahead of me, helping me.

Look for His help every day. Listen for the marching feet in the poplars.

Or find *something* that reminds you of your Father's words: "I am here to help you."

And one more example—

As the Israelites prepared to cross the Jordan River into the Promised Land, Moses warned them that they were going to face stiff resistance. It was a good land, but the people who had been settled there for generations were strong and powerful, descendants of giants, and their cities were well fortified. It looked like a rough road ahead for the refugees from Egypt.

"But," said Moses,

"Recognize today that the LORD your God is the one who will cross over ahead of you like a devouring fire to destroy them. He will subdue them so that you will quickly conquer them and drive them out, just the LORD has promised." (Deuteronomy 9:3)

Recognize this. Know this: The Lord has made promises to you, and He goes before you to keep His promises.

Later, Moses repeated the encouragement:

"So be strong and courageous! Do not be afraid and do not panic before them. For the LORD your God will personally go ahead of you. He will neither fail you nor abandon you." (Deuteronomy 31:6)

Those are all words for us, too. Our God is the same God, one who will not abandon His children.

Recognize that He goes before you. Do not be afraid of problems and conflict and seemingly impossible situations, insurmountable odds, or unconquerable opposition. Do not panic. The Lord your God has made promises to you and will not fail to keep them. So go forward, strong and courageous.

After all, He's torn open the heavens to be with you and help you.

⸓⸓⸓ LIVING MYSTERIES ⸓⸓⸓

You are witnesses that I am the only God.
- from ISAIAH 43:12 -

And you will be my witnesses,
telling people about me everywhere...
- from ACTS 1:8 -

During an especially dark time in my life, I was just hanging on by my fingernails. I couldn't see much further than the next hour or two, and I needed reassurance that I could get through each long day. You may be at just such a point in your own life—struggling to put one foot in front of another and keep going.

Trying to drag myself through each day wasn't working well, so I began combing through the Scriptures, looking for help, searching for any whisper that somehow it was possible to find new light and strength and help.

And I found not whispers, but loud, robust, joyful declarations! Scripture offers so much reassurance. God wants us to know Him and to know that He is here to help us. Jesus came to help us, because we needed help. Long before I was born, He prayed for me (John 17)! And He is still my advocate before God. Scripture tells us that God is always saying to His children, "I am here to help you."

I survived that time, with God's help. Now I'm beginning to see that there is much more to God's plan than for Him to simply help me survive trouble and hard times.

When you are crawling through a hard time, I know it's difficult to see anything more than the obstacles, tangled messes, and dark paths in front of you, and it's almost impossible to feel or think about anything other than the pain. But bear with me. Read this meditation now, and come back to it later, when the light shines a little brighter on a smoother path.

Know that God has promised that you can live today with expectation.

You can even expect joy.

Oh. I know that can seem like an impossible dream. But joy does come. And it comes from something far greater than surviving our crises.

One of the passages I have read and re-read is the first part of Isaiah 43. I have often needed to hear those verses that promise that even as I go through the worst of trouble, God will be with me, holding me, comforting me, taking care of me. I will always be in His hands because I am precious to Him.

Those first verses in Isaiah 43 record God's words to His people, saying, "Do not be afraid. You are mine. I'll always be with you. When you go through deep waters, you will not drown. When you walk through fire, you will not be burned up. You are precious to me. Don't be afraid. I am with you."

He was speaking at that time to the nation of Israel, but we have the same God who makes the same promises to hold His children in His care. We, too, can cling to those words.

But let's go on further into the chapter, past the opening verses of fire and flood.

Then we find that God's people have a high calling. They have been rescued and chosen to know God and believe in Him and to *stand as witnesses that He exists and is the only God.*

As we read the entire chapter, we see that the people of Israel were just like us: not at all perfect. Sometimes wandering too far away from God. Getting themselves into trouble. Needing God's rescue. They did not always live as "God's people." Yet, they belonged to Him. He claimed them. He had a purpose for them.

God says the same things to His people today, those He has adopted as His children. He has rescued us, promises to hold us through everything we have to go through on this earth, and tells us that we are to stand as living testimony that He is alive and He is God.

As Jesus gives instructions to those who follow Him, we hear Him using the same word: *Be my witnesses.* Jesus sent the first disciples into the world to tell the world about Him. He sends everyone who believes in Him on the same mission. *Tell the world who I am and what I can do.*

I want my life to stand as testimony that God exists and lives in me. I am not the person I used to be, and the only explanation I have for that miraculous, mysterious change is that God is alive and is doing what He promised He would do.

God doesn't pull us out of this world and move us to a perfect place as soon as we say we believe in Him. He doesn't put us on a road that is always smooth and free of danger. He doesn't wrap us in shrink wrap so that nothing can touch us. Nor are we instantly, magically free of old attitudes and behaviors. But His divine, incredible power, that goes far beyond disaster and evil, holds us and helps us and teaches us and re-creates us.

So as we go forward and look at God's promises of rescue today, keep this in mind: He's chosen us. He loves us. He's gone to great lengths to make us His children. And we are to stand, even in fire and flood, as witnesses to His love and power and to who He is and what He does.

THIS IS THE LORD'S DOING!

This is the LORD's doing, and it is wonderful to see.
— PSALM 118:23 —

Do you remember that chorus so many of us learned as children? "This is the day the LORD has made. We will rejoice and be glad in it."

That's from Psalm 118, from a series of verses that Jesus quoted. He didn't sing the catchy little chorus. He quoted those Scriptures when He was trying to help His listeners understand that God was beginning a new covenant with people, opening a new way—making a new day, in which people could rejoice and be glad.

That verse is preceded by the verse above, declaring that the Lord has done this, and it's wonderful to see.

Both verses refer to not just one day, but to the greatest help God has ever given to humankind—

sending Jesus to clear the barrier between us and God and heal our relationship with our Creator. A new day had come. That was the good news Jesus brought. God had done it, and it was wonderful!

May I suggest that we adapt the above verse to our everyday lives? As the Lord helps us through our days, in small and miraculous ways, could this be our song?

Betty and I lived through the storm. The Lord brought us through, and it was wonderful.

I held my tongue that night in the difficult conversation. It was all the Lord's doing.

That crazy, overbooked week of deadlines and commitments, when I was overwhelmed because I'd overpromised—it was God who smoothed my road.

I am a new person. The old is fading away, the new is constantly growing stronger. The Lord is doing it, and it's wonderful.

Look for it. Find something in every day that is evidence of God, coming to help you, and say to yourself and others, *That is the Lord's doing. It's wonderful to see!*

That's how we stand as witnesses to our God.

For more promises of God's help,
see the appendix for a list of additional Scriptures.

PRAYER FOR NEW STRENGTH:

Look down and have mercy on me.

Give strength to your servant.

– **PSALM 86:16** –

FINDING NEW STRENGTH

FOR THOSE WHO TRUST

But those who trust in the LORD will find new strength.

- from ISAIAH 40:31 -

Do you feel as if you can bear no more?

Have you crossed the threshold that marks the limit of your patience or endurance or love or forgiveness?

Have you been given a task that is too much for you?

Is the mountain simply too high and steep?

Are you drained of all will to continue on the path?

If any of those questions hit a mark in your heart and soul, have you heard this hope?

Those who trust in the LORD will find new strength. (Isaiah 40:31)

He gives power to the weak, and strength to the powerless. (Isaiah 40:29)

To those who do not know that the everlasting God, Creator of all the earth and heavens, is also a loving Father who provides for the needs of His children, this will seem like a foolish and futile hope. But as I search the words of my Father, this promise pops up as frequently as the promise that He'll always be ready to help.

I so often need this promised new strength. To my mind, *new* means more than just a refreshment of my own fortitude. It means strength beyond anything I've known before—new limits to what I can bear, new levels of vigor, new depth of endurance, new ability to do what I could not do before. The strength He gives goes beyond my mortal resources.

Does all that sound incredible?

It is incredible. And it's a promise from the God who keeps His promises.

The LORD is the everlasting God, the Creator of all the earth. He gives power to the weak and strength to the powerless. Even youths will become weak and tired, and young men will fall in exhaustion. But those who trust in the LORD will find new strength. They will soar high on wings like eagles. They will run and not grow weary. They will walk and not faint. (Isaiah 40:28-31)

You're probably quite familiar with this passage. It outlines the promise of new strength. But right now, I'm asking if you believe this promise. Will you dare to go forward over this bridge of hope, knowing that God will make this happen? Trusting that you are going to find new strength?

Ask, and you'll receive, Jesus said. *Seek, and you'll find.*

This promise is for those who trust in the Lord's provision for His children. If you do trust Him, you can go right to Him whenever you need a strength you've never experienced before... and you'll find it and receive it.

ᔓᔐᔑᖋ LOOKING FOR COMMITTED HEARTS ᖋᔑᔐᔓ

The eyes of the LORD search the whole earth in order to strengthen those whose hearts are fully committed to him.
— from 2 CHRONICLES 16:9 —

King Asa of Judah saw trouble ahead—the probable invasion of his country by a far more powerful nation.

Looking for help against the enemy, Asa made an alliance with the king of Aram. He even took all the silver and gold from the Temple treasury to pay for this support.

You would think, perhaps, that God would be angry that His Temple had been emptied of silver and gold. But listen to what God says to Asa through a messenger: "You have been a fool. You put your trust in the king of Aram instead of in me. As a result, you have lost the opportunity I would have given you to completely wipe out the enemy. So now the enemy still exists and wars will continue."

Asa's biggest mistake was to trust someone else other than God.

The messenger also tells King Asa something we all need to remember: The Lord is looking for those hearts fully committed to Him. He's searching them out, specifically to pour His strength into them. (See the opening verse.)

Isn't this a comfort to you? It is to me. That makes life more exciting—and hope-full.

Remember the definitions of *committed?*

One is *giving something in trust, entrusting for safekeeping.* If we've committed our hearts to God, trusting Him with our hearts and souls and lives, we've put everything in His hands.

A second definition is *to bind or pledge oneself to.* Again, He says that those who have pledged themselves to Him are those He is seeking to strengthen.

But King Asa had committed to a neighboring king. He'd given his trust, the security of his country, and his pledge to the king of Aram instead of to the God of Israel—and so he forfeited a great victory God would have given him.

I wonder how many times we miss great victories because we trust in our own resources or in other people—instead of trusting God to give us strength for the battle we're facing.

When we need *new* strength, do we go immediately to the Lord? Or is our first action to call our best friend, our counselor, or our pastor in hopes that they can give us the boost and courage we need?

Like King Asa, we strip riches from our spiritual storehouses when we do not go to our Father for His help and strength. What do we lose? We miss the opportunities to learn more about His strength, to strengthen our trust in Him, and to send our roots more deeply into Him. When we go elsewhere for help instead of to the Father, we cheat ourselves, weakening our faith and limiting our hope.

How might our daily lives change if the first person we went to was our heavenly Father, who promises to strengthen us if we're committed to Him?

He's looking for committed hearts... so that He can work incredibly in their lives.

LIVING ON UNLIMITED RESOURCES

I pray that from his [the Father's] glorious, unlimited resources he will empower you with inner strength through his Spirit.

— EPHESIANS 3:16 —

She used to be my neighbor, but I've moved and don't see her often. I think of her often, though, because her inner strength had such an impact on me.

I had not seen her for almost a year, but I'd heard that doctors had found a disease ravaging her body. She had been told there was no stopping the illness. It would take her life within a year, they said. But when we spent some time together one day, I thought she looked better than I'd ever seen her.

"When they told me what was wrong with me," she told me, "all I could think was, *What am I going to do? What am I going to do?* I knew I'd have to make all kinds of decisions, and I just didn't know how I was going to go through this.

"So I just prayed and prayed and prayed. And one day—it was just as though someone was talking to me—God said everything would be all right. And I quit worrying."

She went on to tell me about facing impossible mountains; God had shrunk them to little piles of dirt in her path. I listened to her stories and thought that I was seeing a jar of clay, a very fragile jar of clay, that was positively glowing with the all-surpassing power of God within.

This, I thought, *is what Ephesians 3:16 means!* Her heart, committed to the Father, had been infused with His glorious, unlimited resources. The Holy Spirit had brought an inner strength to her, and she was shining with strength and peace.

Inner strength. That's what I want. My fragile jar of clay has little to offer on its own, but I want to live *beyond* my fragile self. That's not too much to hope for, is it?

Not for a child of the Almighty.

When I feel at the end of my rope, I don't want to just tie a knot and hold on. I want to throw away the rope and lift up my arms to ask my Father to carry me.

When we feel overwhelmed by circumstances or schedule, His Spirit will help us.

When we are so weak and feel unable to live the life Jesus wants us to live, He will live His life through us as long as we hold onto Him.

When we would rather clutch our bitterness
    instead of forgiving,
when we are too selfish to live love,
when people are so annoying that we lose
    sight of how much God loves them,
when we're tempted to think a situation is
    hopeless...
then we need the power of His resources.

This is the secret: If our hearts are committed to Him, if we are trusting in Him, then we are no longer living this life on our own. The Spirit is living out His life in us. And He brings to us an inner strength that is something far beyond what we could cook up on our own.

This is such good news for me! It means that it's not all up to me. I don't have to somehow dredge up my own scant resources and bolster them in hopes that I've "got what it takes." No. It's not all up to me.

I do have a choice to make. Am I going to call out to God for His help, or will I go running off to other places, looking for other ways to find strength to keep going?

Our hope knows that when we go to God for His resources, He is there to help.

In the middle of a song celebrating God's constant love and His commitment to His people, we find this line:

It pleases [Him] to make us strong. (Psalm 89:17)

He will empower us with strength and inner resources beyond anything we've known before. And it delights Him to do this for us! That's incredible, isn't it? Not only incredible, but beyond explaining or our comprehension. Yet this is what God says is true. It's one of the wonderful, comforting mysteries of being a child of God.

DEEP ROOTS GO TO THE SOURCE

Search for the LORD and for his strength;
continually seek him.
– **PSALM 105:4** –

In the days before David became king of all Israel, he was forced to live for a time in another country.

He and the band of men loyal to him settled there, raising their families in one particular town.

One day, after David and his men had been absent for some time (marching off to a battle), they returned home to find their town burned to the ground and all of their wives and children gone. A neighboring country had raided and destroyed the town, taking everyone captive.

Take a moment to imagine what they must have felt as they came into sight of what had been their homes, now deserted and destroyed.

They wept until they could weep no more. Then anger set in. David suddenly found himself in danger, because his men were bitter about losing their families. They turned their anger on David for taking them away from their homes. There was even talk of killing him. So David not only had to deal with his own overwhelming grief, he was also faced with his men turning against him.

At such a hard time, what would you have done? Where would you have turned?

There's a follow-up to that verse in Ephesians that speaks of God empowering us with His unlimited resources. In the verse following it, we see the result:

Then Christ will make his home in your hearts as you trust in him. Your roots will grow down deep into God's love and keep you strong. (Ephesians 3:17)

Notice that it is not that we *stay strong.* We *are kept* strong. That's so reassuring to me. I know how quickly any strength I drum up on my own can seep away—sometimes, within minutes. I cannot create or sustain real strength on my own. It is His power, not mine, that keeps me strong.

Our strength comes not from ourselves. It's a hard thing for our minds to grasp, conditioned as we are by our culture, thinking that we must be strong and self-sufficient. Yet this is what God says is reality: When we are weak, then His strength flows into us. When the task is too big and the mountain too high, His strength enlivens our hearts. When we are completely emptied of our own resources, then His resources can fill us.

Or, to put it another way, when my heart is drained and emptied of *me,* then Christ can move in and I'll live on *His* resources.

Then we sink our roots deep into the love of Christ. And as our roots go deep into His love, we are kept strong.

How do we send down roots into God's love? Well, how do you become rooted and stand firm in the love of another person? You spend time with them. You are honest and open with them. You share your soul with them. You learn to trust them.

That's also how your roots grow down deep into God's love. And it is that love that will keep you strong.

As a disciple of Jesus, I see Him giving us a powerful example: He often retreated to "a lonely place" to pray and be with His Father. I, too, need time alone with my Father and Teacher. I need that connection to the Source of all strength.

When we seek help elsewhere, and look to someone or something else for our help and rescue, we shut the door of our hearts to Christ and our roots stay shallow, never reaching deeply into God.

Hear Christ's words to us:

"Yes, I am the vine; you are the branches. Those who remain in me, and I in them, will produce much fruit. For apart from me you can do nothing." (John 15:5)

To find power and strength to do anything, we must be connected to the Vine, or, as Paul wrote, sink our roots deep into God's love and open our hearts for Christ to make His home there.

We've used three different metaphors here,

but they all say one thing: our lives must be grounded, rooted, and saturated with Christ's life and love.

Without this connection, Jesus said, we will shrivel up and be powerless. Compare that warning to this confidence:

For I can do everything through Christ,
who gives me strength. (Philippians 4:13)

Our strength depends on our relationship with the Source of strength. There's a prophecy in the book of Daniel about a ruler who will someday bring great persecution upon God's people. *"But the people who know their God will be strong and will resist him"* (Daniel 11:32).

The people who know their God will be strong... They'll have deep roots. They'll be connected to the Vine. They will know that Christ is right at home in them, and it is His resources that keep them going.

I want all of that. I need to know my God!

David knew his God. The account of the raid on his town, the loss of his family, and the mutiny of his men is told in 1 Samuel 30. Tucked into the details of his misery is this line: "But David found strength in the LORD his God." This is the man who later wrote psalm after psalm saying that God was his strength... his only strength.

I want to find the new strength God promises to committed hearts. And when His eyes search the earth for those hearts, does He see mine?

FOR HIS GLORY AND MISSION

May he give you the power to accomplish all the good things your faith prompts you to do. Then the name of our LORD Jesus will be honored because of the way you live...

- **from 2 THESSALONIANS 1:11-12** -

"Could it be that He gives us strength to lead not a life of comfort, but a life of risk and daring for His glory?" This thoughtful question came from a blog I follow, entitled *Everyday Servant.*

It jarred my thinking. Yes, God does provide what we need for a purpose far greater than just getting us through today.

Too often, we can't see beyond the end of our own noses, and when we celebrate our hope of God providing us strength, we're thinking only of our own benefit, of getting through our own hard times.

And He does provide strength, both for our everyday walk and for the trials of fire and flood. We can depend on that. That's one way He cares for and protects His children.

But here's more to think about today:

His strength in us works to achieve His purposes. If I belong to Him, then the purpose of all that I do and all that I am is now to point others toward His glory. That is why I am still here on earth. As He supplies everything I need, it is not only for my own journey, it is also to shine a light toward Home to help others along the way.

Our weakness can bring Him glory. I think of my friend with the terminal illness. She glows with God's strength and peace. I think of another family who is writing their own book of Job. It seems they have been asked to bear much more than most of us. Yet they have an uncommon radiance and vitality in their faith that makes me yearn for the same. I know it has come from their dependence on God. Paul wrote about this: God's power shines through our weakness. When we are weak, then we are strong. When we are weak, then the strength we exhibit points to our God, our rock. We stand as witnesses to His existence and His presence and power in our lives.

He works through us. I believe we're given strength and training in battle not only for ourselves but also to help others in their battles with the enemy. Peter wrote encouragement to use the gifts God has given to each of us: "Use them well to serve one another... do it with all the strength and energy that God supplies. Then everything you do will bring glory to God through Jesus Christ" (1 Peter 4:10, 11).

He gives us strength to live out our call to His mission. Paul was thinking along the same lines when he wrote: "So we keep on praying for you, asking our God to enable you to live a life worthy of his call. May he give you the power to accomplish all the good things your faith prompts you to do. Then the name of our LORD Jesus will be honored because of the way you live..." (from 2 Thessalonians 1:11, 12).

Back in the times of the Jewish exile in Babylon, some of the people had returned to Jerusalem to rebuild the city and the Temple. However, work lagged and eventually stopped as enemies opposed the project. Finally, God sent a message through a prophet: "Be strong and get to work, for I am with you." (See Haggai 2:4)

Could God be saying that to me in some area of my life today? Rather than lamenting the circumstances or my own lack of skill, power, or knowledge, might God want me to get busy so that He can infuse His own resources into my work and others can see Him in my life?

Christ had similar words to His disciples as He sent them out on His mission: "Get going. Bring more people to be my disciples. And I'll always be with you."

As sons and daughters of God, we're now a part of Christ's mission here on earth. "Could it be that He gives us strength to lead not a life of comfort, but a life of risk and daring for His glory?"

STRENGTH AND JOY FOR PILGRIMS

What joy for those whose strength comes from the LORD, who have set their minds on pilgrimage.
(They go from strength to strength, until each appears before God in Zion.)

– from **PSALM 84:5-6** –

We began this section by asking if you're at the end of your resources and ready to give up. Ask yourself now if you will keep on going, over the bridge of this promise that God will provide an inner strength you've never known before.

Jesus said: "According to your faith, it will be done to you."

I want to live with great expectation, knowing that I don't have to simply ride the ebb and tide of what I can accomplish on my own strength, but throwing myself into life, trusting that Jesus' incredible power does work in my life. That's part of my inheritance as a child of God.

I want to say often, "Surely God has done this, and it's wonderful to see!"

How much more joy I find when I come through a tough project, tangled relationship conflict, emotional wilderness, or any other thing for which I don't have the resources, and I know that *God has done this.* Not that I've done it. Not that someone I admire has done it. But what has happened is so outside the expected, possible, and probable that I know *only God could have done this!*

Yes, I want a life filled with all those moments of joy.

> *So may we, you and I, fellow pilgrim, be strengthened with all His glorious power so we will have all the endurance and patience we need. And may we be filled with joy, always thanking our Father.* (paraphrase from Colossians 1:11-12)

Soak up more hope of new strength,
see the appendix for a list of additional Scriptures.

PRAYER WHEN FACING
THE ENEMY:

I look to you for help,

O Sovereign LORD.

You are my refuge.

Don't let them kill me.

– PSALM 141:8 –

WINNING THE BATTLE

◦≺≺∙∿∿ VICTORY PROMISED ∿∿∙≻≻◦

He has given us great and precious promises. These are the
promises that enable you to share his divine nature and
escape the world's corruption caused by human desires.

– from 2 PETER 1:4 –

Are you fighting a battle right now? Perhaps
it's more than a single battle; maybe you're in an
ongoing, years-long war, and you are exhausted
and doubting that there will ever be an end to the
struggle.

Or possibly you are so besieged by forces coming against you that you have given up, thinking that there is no way you will ever have the victory.

You might be wondering, *Where is my God? Why do I constantly have to fight this? Isn't He on my side? Why doesn't He step in and end this?*

Those are all hard questions. And it might even be that the battle has been so long and hard that you find it difficult to read this from God's Word without feeling cynical:

"See, all your angry enemies lie there, confused and humiliated. Anyone who opposes you will die and come to nothing.

You will look in vain for those who tried to conquer you. Those who attack you will come to nothing.

For I hold you by your right hand—I, the LORD *your God. And I say to you, 'Don't be afraid. I am here to help you.'"* (Isaiah 41:11-13)

Those lines sound quite a triumphant note, don't they? But as you read, you may have even felt a jab of bitterness or stubborn doubt.

God promises victory over the enemy. A resounding victory. Chapter 41 in Isaiah goes on to say "you'll be like a threshing instrument with sharp teeth, tearing the enemy apart."

We all wish for such victories, whether our battles are small skirmishes with the enemy or if we're in a long, drawn-out war.

In the book of Psalms, David constantly rejoices that the Lord delivered him from his enemies. And David had plenty of enemies and battles he had to fight. But as we look at the whole body of God's Word to us, we see that God didn't have some special, exclusive arrangement with King David; God will do the same for us, every day in all the hours of our lives.

Take a minute, re-read the opening Scripture, and notice two things that His promises enable us to do...

These promises are just so amazing to me that I had to remind you, too. It's more than we can imagine, right?

It may be difficult to see such hope while you're in the heat of the battle, but know that this is His Word to us, His promise.

So let's take some time to look at what God says about our battles in this world.

THE ENEMY

For we are not fighting against flesh-and-blood enemies,
but against evil rulers and authorities of the unseen world,
against mighty powers in this dark world, and against evil
spirits in the heavenly places.

– EPHESIANS 6:12 –

I felt a certain resistance to typing the verse above. It goes against my desires for this book. I've wanted to open each meditation with verses that speak of promise and hope. And that verse from Ephesians is dark, heavy, and worrisome. I'd rather choose something more positive and uplifting.

And then—perhaps it was a Spirit-suggested thought—it occurred to me that veering away from this verse would be exactly what the enemy wants us to do: he wants us to ignore or downplay what he is trying to do in this world.

That thought settled it. I was determined to use the verse.

We must see, first of all, that the battle is against an enemy who seeks to destroy our souls.

This enemy knows me well. Probably better than I know myself. He knows when I am most vulnerable and when an attack is most likely to be successful. He knows what weapons are most likely to wound and weaken me. He knows what enticements are most likely to lure me off the path.

But it's not me he cares about. Satan's ultimate purpose in this war is to usurp God's rule and destroy God's plan for His creation. He comes after you and me, just as he used Adam and Eve and attempted to use Jesus.

You see what this means: We are not dealing with human enemies. Those people we might view as enemies are caught in Satan's strategies in this war. Our enemies are not other people—those people are just as loved by God as we are! God offers them the same rescue and freedom that He offers us. Even if they've vowed to kill us, those people are not our true enemies. Our true enemies are spiritual powers and beings who are at war with God.

The enemy comes at us in so many and various ways. From the outside: Bombardment by society's values and philosophies. Busy schedules. Temptations. Financial strains. Growing hostility toward Christianity. Conflicts in relationships. And from the inside: Discouragement. Depression. Doubt. Fear. Worry. Stress. Selfishness. Anger. Health concerns.

You know what battles you must constantly fight. What obstacles sometimes loom up and look impossible and overwhelming. The situations you are tempted to call hopeless. The dark parts of your nature that sometimes hold you in a strong grip.

Who can be triumphant in all these battles? What person made of dust can rip apart the spiritual powers of evil?

Every child of God!

Why? Because He has chosen us and will not abandon us. He holds us by the hand and is here to help us. And it is He who fights the battle for us and has promised us victory.

It is the bridge of promise and hope over which our faith moves forward into battle.

THOSE WHO KNOW HIM, TRUST HIM

All the LORD's promises prove true. He is a shield for all who look to him for protection.

– from **PSALM 18:30** –

The enemy was bigger, stronger, and better equipped. To all appearances, their marches to battle seemed futile and fatal. (Have there been times like this in your life?)

Yet the children of Israel won. Decisively.

The opening chapters of the book of 1 Chronicles look like a boring historical account of descendants of descendants of descendants.

You know, one of those *begat* lists that we tend to skim over or skip completely. But there's a line tucked into the fifth chapter about some of the tribes of Israel as they settled in their new land—a line that we need to take notice of:

They cried out to God during the battle, and he answered their prayer because they trusted in him. (1 Chronicles 5:20)

I challenge you today to ask yourself: "How much do I trust God?"

That grand promise by God that we find in Isaiah 41 that our enemies will come to nothing is so full of hope for us flesh-and-blood, dust people. We are fighting evil spiritual powers! We might wonder, *What hope is there for us in this battle?*

This is the hope: God has promised victory.

And so, each one of us has to decide whether we trust this promise. Because if you do not trust the bridge, your faith will certainly not go forward over it.

This quote from Charles Spurgeon gets to the bottom line quickly:

It is the cause of much weakness to many that they do not treat the promises of God as realities. If a friend makes them a promise, they regard it as a substantial thing, and look for that which it secures;

but the declarations of God are often viewed as so many words which means very little. –According to Promise

How much do we trust the promise of God? Do we trust our friend's promise more than we trust God's word to us?

David was a friend of God. He wrote "Those who know your name trust in you" (Psalm 9:10). He knew God's character well, and his confidence and trust in the compassion and protection of the Lord rises from every page of the Psalms.

Here are some of the things David knew for a certainty about the character of his God:

He rescues me from the traps of my enemies. (25:15)

In His unfailing love, my God will stand with me and will give me victory. (59:10)

All the LORD's promises prove true. (18:30)

He is a faithful God. (31:5)

He does not abandon those who search for Him. (9:10)

He is strength and shield. (28:7) (Think about what the word *shield* implies.)

The list could go on and on. On almost every

page in the book of Psalms, we find trust in the reality of the promises of God.

Are we treating the promises of God as reality?

In Isaiah 52:6, the Lord says, *"I will reveal my name to my people, and they will come to know its power."*

If we've come to know the Lord's name—that is, His character, who He is—do our lives reflect that reality? Are we living in the reality of this hope of victory over the enemy?

Remember that Biblical hope is the assurance that what is promised *will* happen.

God says the reality is that His children *will* be victorious.

WHO CAN HAVE THIS VICTORY?

Who can win this battle against the world? Only those who believe that Jesus is the Son of God.

- 1 JOHN 5:5 -

John, one of Jesus' closest friends on this earth, wrote a letter in which he focused on Jesus' commandments, summed up in the command to love: Love God, and love each other.

Jesus said those are the two most important things for us to do. But as we attempt to follow that command, we soon find that pretty much every evil in this world works *against* that kind of love.

This means that evil will be coming against us as we live out Jesus' commandments. But John declares emphatically that every child of God can defeat the evil. There's no waffling or doubt in his hope:

> For every child of God defeats this evil world, and we achieve this victory through our faith. And who can win this battle against the world? Only those who believe that Jesus is the Son of God.
> (1 John 5:4-5)

The phrase "through our faith" reminds me of Jesus' words to people who had come to Him for healing: "Your faith has made you well," He said more than once. Those people who were healed had faith in Jesus' power.

That's where our hope and victory lie, too. We believe that Jesus is the Son of God; we have faith in Him, in His power, in what He teaches us, and in what He has promised to do in our lives. That faith will be what enables us to defeat the evil that would infect and destroy us.

Jesus said that we would have trouble in this world, but promised that His power was greater than any other power we'd meet. He told us that

His power had broken all evil powers. How do we live in that reality?

If we are putting our faith in Him, then we look to Him for answers, help, and examples. We pattern our lives after His. We trust what He tells us. Is there a better place to look for help than to the Son of God?

Jesus stepped into our history to help men and women like you and me. He became like us "in every way," the writer of Hebrews tells us. We forget that sometimes. We forget that as a man He experienced all the human needs and desires and frustrations and disappointments and stuff of daily living that we do.

Since He lived a human life, He has, like us, been caught in the troubles of this world and the battles between God's good and Satan's evil.

Some of Jesus' most powerful lessons for us were not in His sermons or His parables but in His own human struggles. Through His battles against the evil, He gave us examples of how to fight—and win. Let's take two instances when Jesus was in a fierce battle with spiritual enemies coming against His humanity. We can identify with these because we find ourselves in the same battles today.

What did He do? How did He fight the battle?

The first example Jesus gave us is found in Matthew 16. Jesus' popularity was still high. Great crowds were coming to hear Him teach. Peter had made that declaration of his belief that Jesus was the Son of God.

Then, abruptly and to the dismay of His friends, Jesus started talking about what lay ahead for Him—death at the hands of the religious leaders. It was God's plan, and it was going to happen soon.

Shaken, Peter started to argue. "That can't happen! Don't even talk like that!" he said.

Jesus got rather sharp with His dear friend Peter. Could it be He responded so harshly because the temptation was so strong? Did Jesus feel the same thoughts rising up within Himself? Was He fighting a desire to abandon His mission and say "Forget it, I don't want to do this"? Do you suppose Peter's comment added to the power of the temptation Jesus was already fighting? Is that why Jesus' response was so sharp? He even said, "Get away from me, Satan!" If I would have been Peter, that comment from my friend would have stung.

Jesus' tone softened a bit as He explained: *"You are a dangerous trap to me. You are seeing things merely from a human point of view, not from God's"* (Matthew 16:23).

Do you catch the significance of that? Jesus admitted He was looking into a dangerous trap. He acknowledged that He was standing at a fork in His path—one way was God's way; the other way followed natural, human thinking and needs, a way that any one of us would say is "logical." Jesus was fully human, just like us. He must have felt the same resistance we would feel at the prospect of a humiliating, brutal death. Remember how He struggled in Gethsemane the night before His arrest? His prayer then shows that He would have welcomed an adjustment to God's plan of a sacrificial death. Jesus was very human!

So when His good friend voiced a desire for Jesus to somehow avoid that death and find an alternate path, Jesus acknowledged that the trap was real and dangerous. He was tempted!

Our prayer can be, *Lord Jesus, when a trap lies ready to clamp its jaws around me at my next step, give me a glimpse of God's point of view and God's reality.*

The second example Jesus gave us was when He hung on the cross, dying. At the very last, He cried out, "Father, into your hands I commit my spirit."

He was quoting a well-known psalm. David wrote the original line, and it was set in the context of David's own faith in a time of battle, seeking protection from the traps of evil.

As Jesus, a human being like us, hung there dying, we know from His own words that He thought God had forsaken Him. In His last moments, after He had agonized so painfully over what He must do and had prayed for strength to carry it through... it seemed God had deserted Him.

What must He have felt?

How would you feel, if you've given up so much to follow what you thought was God's plan and will for you—and then, it seems that God deserts you. You cannot feel God's presence or His power and blessing. It seems as though evil has won. How would you feel?

Jesus' prayer with His last breath is a prayer for us when we feel overwhelmed, when we feel God is not beside us, when we cannot see the hope or God's point of view, when, to our eyes, we are doomed to lose the battle.

Then, the only thing we can do is simply to say as Jesus did in those terrible moments, *Father, hold me. My faith is slipping. My strength is gone. I give myself into Your hands. Hold me.*

Two powerful examples for us. The God who

came as a human being to help us, because we need help, fought battles Himself and showed us ways to have victory over all the evil that comes against us.

Jesus has much more to teach us. And if we believe in Him—if we believe He *is* the Son of God—and we have faith in all He teaches us?

Then the promise is that we *will* win the battle.

⟫⟫ OUR REAL POWER ⟪⟪

Only by your power can we push back our enemies, only in your name can we trample our foes. I do not trust in my bow; I do not count on my sword to save me. You are the one who gives us victory over our enemies.

– PSALM 44:5-7 –

Might it be that we stunt the growth of our faith with a simple choice of words?

Even as we talk of resisting the devil and of defeating the enemy, has he cleverly twisted our thinking to keep our faith from growing?

I'm talking about our use of the small pronouns *I, me, and we.*

When I focus on what *I must do,* on what *I can do,* to gain victory in this great battle, then Satan has already clamped a shackle around my faith.

Because my faith and hope wither quickly when I'm focused only on *my* strength and resources.

When our faith is struggling to believe, let it shift its focus to the one who makes all the difference in this battle—Jesus, the Rescuer.

The one to whom all authority has been given.

The one who broke the power of evil and sin.

The one whose Spirit lives with His followers as a Helper.

The apostle Paul wrote quite a bit about how Satan uses the feelings and attitudes of our old nature to trap us and lead us down paths the children of God should never walk. Paul wrote of his own great struggles against the enemy. But he also wrote these encouragements:

> *Because you belong to [Christ Jesus], the power of the life-giving Spirit has freed you from the power of sin that leads to death.* (Romans 8:2)

> *So I say, let the Holy Spirit guide your lives. Then you won't be doing what your sinful nature craves.* (Galatians 5:16)

> *The Holy Spirit helps us in our weakness.* (Romans 8:26)

You're probably familiar with the inspirational

piece written about footsteps in the sand. A man, looking back on his life, sees how God had carried him through the toughest times, when he couldn't walk himself.

It would not surprise me to find, someday in the future when I can see all things clearly, that there have been terrible battles raging about me in the spiritual world, battles I've been unaware of. Perhaps all I knew at the time (in my limited wisdom) was that I was having a terrible day or that I was struggling with doubt or depression or temptation or pain or anger. But in those frays, even though I never saw it or felt it, Jesus' Spirit was fighting for me.

Scriptures say that the Spirit prays for us, even when we cannot pray ourselves. I believe the Spirit fights for us, too, when we are discouraged and exhausted by the ferocity of the battle, when we do not know how to fight, and even when we are unaware of the attack.

John wrote this encouragement:

The Spirit who lives in you is greater than the spirit who lives in the world. (1 John 4:4)

Doesn't that remind you of Jesus' words that He has overcome the world?

All who believe become children of God, and the

Helper comes to live with every child of God. His power is greater than any evil power in the world.

There lies the secret of victory and peace even during the hardest battles. It has nothing to do with our own strength or resources. For all who believe in the Son of God, there's an incredible power at work for us. That's our real power against the strong enemies who come against us.

GOING TO THE THRONE FOR HELP

My enemies will retreat when I call to [God] for help.
This I know: God is on my side!
– **PSALM 56:9** –

We've been speaking in general terms of the "enemy" and the "battles." We all may be facing different battles at the moment, but let's remind ourselves that the source of everything that comes against the children of God is the enemy of God, Satan, the enemy of our souls.

So no matter what battles we are fighting, we need help—we made-of-dust people who are facing powers of the spirit realm.

And the one who can help us sits on the throne, holding ultimate power over all of heaven and earth.

Do you know what you will first meet when

you come to the throne room of the Almighty to ask for help?

What happens when we go to Him for help, especially during a time of testing? If our faith is under fire, if we're ready to cave to the temptation and we know it, what can we expect if we call for help?

> *[Jesus] understands our weaknesses, for he faced all of the same testings we do, yet he did not sin. So let us come boldly to the throne of our gracious God. There we will receive his mercy, and we will find grace to help us when we need it most.* (Hebrews 4:15-16)

Take time to ponder what these words tell us. Take it apart, bit by bit.

Jesus understands our weaknesses because He struggled with the same things. And at times when we are most in danger of giving up the battle, if we go boldly to God we are met first and foremost with mercy.

Mercy!

Here I am, exhausted, my faith teetering, my devotion ready to disintegrate and give up the fight. Yet if I come to Him for help, I meet not judgment or condemnation or a sound scolding, but mercy.

We never need to feel too weak or ashamed or unworthy to ask for His help. We will always be met by His gracious, loving, compassionate kindness because He understands our weakness.

And He comes to help us.

So we need have no doubt or hesitation. As Paul wrote to the Philippians, pray about everything. Tell God what you need. And remember the things He has already done for you (see Philippians 4:6-7). You'll find His compassion and kindness.

He has told us repeatedly,

"I hold you by your right hand—I, the LORD your God. And I say to you, 'Don't be afraid. I am here to help you.'" (Isaiah 41:13)

⤞⤝ TRAINING FOR BATTLE ⤞⤝

It pleases [Him] to make us strong.
- from PSALM 89:17 -

I have to admit that I like the picture: My foot on the neck of my enemies. Destroying all who hate me. Grinding them up as fine as dust and sweeping them into the gutter like dirt. I like it, even though I grew up in the Mennonite pacifist tradition and today I believe even more strongly in Jesus' way of non-violence.

I like the picture because as I read the verses

in Psalm 18 describing this scene, I long for such victories over my spiritual enemies, those powers that hate God and are out to destroy my soul. I do want to see them ground up and blown away like dirt. I want my foot on their neck!

I want Psalm 18 to be a model for my own warfare.

The song begins with wonderful, confident words:

> *I love you, L*ORD*, you are my strength.*
> *The L*ORD *is my rock, my fortress, and my*
> *savior; my God is my rock, in whom I find*
> *protection.* (Psalm 18:1,2)

But things weren't always so good, as we find out by reading further. There were bad times, fearful times, desperate times:

> *The ropes of death entangled me; floods*
> *of destruction swept over me. The grave*
> *wrapped its ropes around me; death laid a*
> *trap in my path.* (verses 4,5)

Sound familiar? I can recall similar feelings at a certain time of my life. Trapped by the enemy. Tangled in ropes of death. Feeling weak and defeated, a captive who had lost the battle. Have you had times of such paralyzing distress?

> *But in my distress I called out to the L*ORD*;*
> *yes, I prayed to my God for help.* (verse 6)

God heard, and the result was dramatic. He came thundering from His sanctuary to reach down and rescue the one in trouble "from those who hated me and were too strong for me." Those were the psalmist's words. Those are my words, too! God did it, and it was wonderful to see!

But wait... there's more to the chapter, and more to our hope:

> *God arms me with strength, and he makes my way perfect. He makes me as surefooted as a deer, enabling me to stand on mountain heights. He trains my hands for battle; he strengthens my arm to draw a bronze bow. You have given me your shield of victory. Your right hand supports me; your help has made me great. You have made a wide path for my feet to keep them from slipping.* (verses 32-36)

God is teaching us to fight this great battle, and He's arming us with the strength to do it.

The next verses create the picture of resounding victory over those enemies who at one time overwhelmed us, held us captive, and were intent on destroying us. Now we chase them down, grind them up like dust, and blow them away.

Oh, yes. That's what I want in my own warfare. Jesus has rescued me. Now I want more than rescue—I want to turn around and chase the enemy to their defeat. I want to do battle with His strength.

That may seem like an impossible thing to you right now, caught in the furor of whatever battle you're in. But this is part of our hope for today: The battle will not only be won, but we will learn to be stronger and stronger against our enemies.

My hope also believes that we're given strength and training to fight not only for our own souls but on behalf of others who are under attack from the same enemies we have battled and known.

Each of us has become intimately familiar with particular strategies of the enemy—we can use that knowledge to help others in their battles.

For example, I know how Satan whispers reminders about my past to keep me from celebrating all the new that God is doing in my life. I understand when someone else is shackled by their past. Jesus had to cut off those same shackles in my own life.

I have a friend who knows from her own experience how the enemy can use depression to try to keep God's children in prison. She can help others who are fighting those battles.

Another friend has lost his spouse to cancer, and he has found a ministry to those traveling through the same grief.

Is it possible that in whatever the enemy is attacking you with right now, God might also be training you to help others in their similar fight?

⤙⤚ SONGS IN OUR CAMP ⤙⤚

Songs of joy and victory are sung in the camp of the godly. The strong right arm of the LORD has done glorious things!
– **PSALM 118:15** –

Jesus tells all of His disciples: "You're going to run into trouble. The world's going to throw a lot at you. Hostility. Heartache. Heavy loads."

Does it mean [Christ] no longer loves us if we have trouble or calamity, or are persecuted, or hungry, or destitute, or in danger, or threatened with death? No, despite all these things, overwhelming victory is ours through Christ, who loved us. (Romans 8:35, 37)

The key to our victory is Jesus Christ, no matter what comes at us. His words in John 14, 15, and 16 are farewell instructions to the eleven disciples (although they don't know yet that it is a farewell), and He lays down a solid path to peace and victory, even though He would be physically absent in the coming days.

Here we also find our path to peace and victory. Jesus tells us so many things in these three chapters.

"Trust me," He says. "Trust God. And following me will bring you to God.

"I'm going away for a while, but I'll be back.

"Remember what I've taught you about loving each other.

"Listen to the Helper I'm going to send. He'll help you to remember what I've said, and He'll teach you, too.

"Stay close to me. Stay connected to me.

"Don't be shocked when the world hates you. It hates me, too.

"Yes, there will be suffering, tears, and trouble, but fantastic joy will come after that.

"And take heart. Don't give up. Because I have overcome the world."

Those words were also spoken for us today. What do they mean to you?

I'm still asking to be taught everything Jesus was saying with those words. I imagine it will take all of life and death until I understand fully. Every time I read through those chapters, the Spirit teaches me something new.

I don't know what battles you're fighting now. I don't know what victory will look like for you.

But I do know this: Jesus said He holds supreme power. Over anything and everything that life in this world throws at you. He promises His strength will flow into you, strength greater than the enemy's. He promises victory. Our Psalm prayer for this section reminds us of His ultimate power and authority: *I look to you for help, O Sovereign LORD.*

So when Jesus says to take heart because He holds victory, we can be certain that is the reality of heaven, where the children of God are living *right now.* We are citizens of a kingdom where our King trumps all other powers and His plan will not be derailed by anyone or anything. It pleases Him to make us strong! And I want to stay so closely connected to my King that I can live according to the realities of His kingdom.

And may songs of joy and victory be sung in our camp, fellow pilgrims, as we tell of the glorious things our God does on behalf of His children.

For more promises of victory,
see the appendix for a list of additional Scriptures.

PRAYER FOR A MORE JOYFUL LIFE:

Show me the way of life, granting me the joy of your presence, and the pleasures of living with you forever.

– Adapted from PSALM 16:11 –

RESCUE FROM AN EMPTY LIFE

MUCH MORE THAN "JUST ENOUGH"

The thief's purpose is to steal and kill and destroy. My purpose is to give them a rich and satisfying life.

- Jesus speaking, JOHN 10:10 -

We've been thinking about troubles and battles and needing help. To now talk about a rich and satisfying life might seem like shifting to an idealistic fantasy.

We are all too acquainted with the difficulties of our journey through this world. That's probably why you picked up this book in the first place. We need help getting through each day. Too often, Jesus' promise of a rich, abundant life seems out of our reach.

So wouldn't it be logical to save this promise for the end of the book—once we know all the promises that we can boldly ask God to fulfill? After our faith has grown more robust and we're living the reality of all this hope? After we have "everything" in place and life is, well, perfect? Then we could talk about a rich and satisfying life, right?

Maybe. But in the Scriptures, we often find *joy* right smack dab in the middle of *trouble.*

And the rich life Jesus has for us is not when we've reached some impossible *perfect* faith. It's for *right now.* We're living in heaven's reality right now, no matter what's going on in the world's reality.

So let's take a look at this hope Jesus gives us.

During Jesus' last supper with His disciples, when He knew events leading to His death were going to unfold swiftly over the next hours, we nevertheless hear Him making frequent mention of *joy.* Jesus was presenting troubling and scary news to His disciples, yet He said, "I'm telling you these things so you'll be filled with joy. Overflowing joy!"

Do you suppose, since they were so much like us, that a few of them were a bit dubious?

Yet they had heard this promise from Him before.

Jesus had talked to them (and us) at length about being a shepherd to His flock. He warned against thieves who come to steal our contentment, to destroy our safety and our lives. But as the Shepherd of our souls, He assures us that He not only keeps us safe but "I've come to give my flock a rich and satisfying life." He came to care for His flock like the shepherd of Psalm 23, providing everything needed for a protected, satisfied, contented life.

The King James version translates Jesus' words as "I've come that they may have life and have it in abundance." Many of us memorized John 10:10 in that version. It's another one of those verses that we might gloss over because it's so familiar. *Don't.* Instead, take time to think deeply about what it means to you to have life "in abundance."

Or, if you're using the NLT, as I did, what does that phrase *rich and satisfying* mean to you?

If you're having trouble putting this into your own words, let's go to the dictionary for help. There, we find *abundant* defined with words like *more than adequate, oversufficient,* and *richly supplied.*

Choose the word or phrase that most resonates with you and tuck it into your mind as you think about Jesus coming into our world. He came to rescue us, yes. But He came to do more than that—He came to give us a life of this overflowing, satisfying, abundant, generous fullness. *More than enough. Richly supplied. Oversufficient.*

Peter wrote that God paid a great ransom, the blood of His Son, to save us from empty lives. (See 1 Peter 1:18)

We don't need the dictionary to help us think about the phrase *empty lives.*

Ponder the comparison of those two words: *abundant* and *empty.*

Does one word bring a smile to your heart because you know God is pouring abundantly into your life?

Or does the other word touch an ache and longing in your soul?

ᵔᵕᶜᵔ FEASTS ARE READY! ᵔᵕᶜᵔ

The LORD is my shepherd. I have all that I need.
- **PSALM 23:1** -

David grew up as a shepherd. He knew that the lives of the sheep depended on the protection, providence, and guidance of the shepherd. As he contemplated the completeness of God's care for His people, the image that came to his mind was that of a shepherd who provides everything his flock needs.

While most of us aren't shepherds, our hearts still translate Psalm 23 into imagery we do understand. Longing for rest and refreshment, we have some sense of what it means to lie down in green pastures, beside still waters. We know the need for guidance and comfort. We feel the fear of evil and the trepidation when facing the shadow of death.

When Jesus said He came to give us a rich and satisfying life, His words echoed what David said about the heavenly Father: "The LORD is my shepherd. I have all that I need."

While we all yearn for the peace, comfort, and assurance of Psalm 23, how many of us would sincerely say those first words? *I have all that I need.*

To our loss, our sights are too often set at ground level. Let's understand that the rich life

Jesus' was talking about is quite different from what the world would say is a rich and satisfying life. The gifts of life He gives us now, while we still walk this earth as His children and live in these bodies and fight the enemy daily, are gifts from the heavenly realm, for life in the kingdom now.

Here's one verse from Psalm 23 that I have learned is full of hope:

"You prepare a feast for me in the presence of my enemies."

Even when all kinds of troubles come into our lives and in the face of all enemies that besiege us in this world and seek to destroy the life God gives us, still our Lord prepares us a feast of blessings and says, "Come, sit down, partake, enjoy, delight—go ahead, *feast*—in everything I have for you."

This is the hope we are confident of, the hope that makes it possible to walk into the unknown future unafraid and even eagerly: When the Lord is our Shepherd, He provides all we need for a full and joyful life. He promises us all the blessings of heaven's reality, even now, on this earth.

Are your feet itching to dance as you shout *Amen!,* or are you grumbling to yourself that this sounds like a bunch of Christian mumbo-jumbo and religious hype?

Let's talk more about it.

❧ TASTE AND SEE ❧

*Taste and see that the LORD is good. Oh, the joys of those
who take refuge in him!*
– **PSALM 34:8** –

Most of the Psalms were songs written for worship in ancient Israel, and they point us to God to find joy and fulfillment and satisfaction and stability in life. The Scriptures speak to all times and cultures; and today, no matter what the current "buzz" words are for those deep needs that drive our lives, the living Word always sends us to one place to find what we seek: *the LORD, the source of all my joy* (Psalm 43:4).

The hearts of those who seek the LORD will rejoice with everlasting joy (Psalm 22:26)

A single day with the LORD is better than a thousand living the "good life" elsewhere (Psalm 84:10)

I desire you more than anything on earth (Psalm 73:25)

You satisfy me more than the richest feast... (Psalm 63:5)

I wonder, though, what refrains we might hear if we listen to the "songs" we are writing by our lives today. What things are we pursuing and looking toward to satisfy our longings and hopes? What do we desire more than anything on earth?

The creation's tendency is, sadly, to wander away from the Creator, looking for joy and satisfaction elsewhere. Satan coaxed Eve into believing the lie that the best life is found outside of God's path, and we've been falling for the same lie ever since. Each generation has a slightly different version, but it always goes something like this: "God can't be trusted to tell you the truth. It's better to become like God yourself, be smart, and decide for yourself. *There's something better than God and God's way.*"

We chase after the wrong things, too. The song that I've always thought says it best is the old hymn that prays, "Bind my wandering heart to Thee" because I am so "prone to wander." ("Come, Thou Fount of Every Blessing" by Robert Robinson)

Hungry hearts yearn to be able to sing some of those lines from the psalms that talk of overflowing joy and sumptuous feasts. Our country even built the pursuit of this ultimate satisfaction into the foundations of its freedom, although we've found that neither constitution or legislation or government declaration can deliver what we're looking for.

When we look to the wrong things and places to put our trust, make us complete, and give us satisfaction, we end up, as the Scripture says, eating ashes (Isaiah 44:20). We are disappointed, we're left with a bad taste in our mouths, and we are never satisfied.

We sing a line of song every year during the Christmas season, but I wonder if our hearts have been thrilled by the truth of what we're singing when we repeat the well-known words of "Joy to the World." Ponder these lines especially:

> *No more let sins and sorrow grow,*
> *Nor thorns infest the ground.*
> *He comes to make His blessings flow*
> *Far as the curse is found.*

That's joy for the world! We are still traveling through this earthly dimension, but heaven's blessings, all of God's goodness and favor, flow into our lives, against the curse of sin and sorrow.

The One who is the Truth-teller has given us a trustworthy lifeline: Our wandering, hungry hearts can find real and lasting satisfaction only in Him. He promised that those who come to Him will never be hungry again. He said He came to bring *life.* The most satisfying, richest, fullest, most complete life you can ever imagine. Even more than you can imagine.

If you've found the Source of all joy and abundance, hold tightly!

If you are still looking, or if you've had enough of eating ashes, or if you scoff and doubt, then maybe you want a taste—to see for yourself what God offers?

EMPTY LIVES FILLED

You will live in joy and peace.
- from ISAIAH 55:12 -

What I desperately wanted was to be rid of the thorns and nettles. I longed for the cypress and myrtle.

That may sound like a strange wish. But it's from a passage I found in Isaiah, a book that gave me much hope in a time of desolation.

Isaiah wrote a great deal about waywardness, wandering, outright rebellion, punishment, and disaster. That was right where I was. But he wrote even more about hope, joy, rescue, transformation, and newness—and that was exactly what I wanted.

God is a god of joy and hope and restoration and new life. The opening Scripture from Isaiah reflects God's ultimate plan for the lives of His people. While I can't quote the entire book of Isaiah here, I'd like to point you to a sampling of His promises. Some of these words were for the Jewish exiles in Babylon, some are also for us today, and some look forward to the new country of our homeland, waiting for us.

If you're wandering and hungry, I'd like you to know that there is much hope in the promises of Scripture.

For anyone who wants to leave an empty life and find a full one, Jesus makes it possible.

I won't comment further on these lines. I simply wish for you to hear the character of our Father and the richness of life He offers us. (Those lines in italics are direct quotes from the New Living Translation; those not italicized are slightly paraphrased.)

Soon the deaf will hear words read from a book, the blind will see through the gloom, the humble will be filled with fresh joy from the LORD, the poor will rejoice, and evil and arrogant people will disappear. (Isaiah 29:18-21)

Comfort my people, speak tenderly to Jerusalem, tell her that her sad days are gone. (Isaiah 40:1,2)

Those who have been ransomed by the

LORD will return. They will enter Jerusalem singing, crowned with everlasting joy. Sorrow and mourning will disappear, and they will be filled with joy and gladness. (Isaiah 51:11)

God says, "Thirsty? Come drink of what I have to give you. Don't spend money on that which does not give you strength. Come, listen to me, and you'll find life and everlasting love." (Isaiah 55:1-3)

You will live in joy and peace. The mountains and hills will burst into song, and the trees of the field will clap their hands! Where once there were thorns, cypress trees will grow. Where there were nettles, myrtles will sprout up. (Isaiah 55:12,13) (Cypress is a symbol of strength and endurance and new life; myrtle was used for perfumes and seasoning. Think about this metaphor of God changing your life. You'll see why I longed for cypress and myrtle instead of thorns and nettles.)

To all who mourn in Israel, he will give a crown of beauty for ashes, a joyous blessing instead of mourning, festive praise instead of despair. (Isaiah 61:3a)

Instead of shame and dishonor, you will enjoy a double share of honor. You will possess a double portion of prosperity in your land, and everlasting joy will be yours. (Isaiah 61:7)

*I am overwhelmed with joy in the L*ORD *my God! For he has dressed me with the clothing of salvation and draped me in a robe of righteousness.* (Isaiah 61:10)

*The L*ORD *will comfort Israel again and have pity on her ruins. Her desert will blossom like Eden, her barren wilderness like the garden of the L*ORD. *Joy and gladness will be found there. Songs of thanksgiving will fill the air.* (Isaiah 51:3)

To prisoners God says, "Come out to freedom." To those in darkness, "Come into the light." Be His sheep, grazing in green pastures on hills that were previously bare. You will not hunger or thirst in His care. He will lead you beside refreshing waters. He'll make mountains into level paths for you. (Isaiah 49:9-11)

Can you hear His offer?

⤳⤳ BEYOND OUR TEASPOONS ⤶⤶

You [O, God] feed them from the abundance of your own house, letting them drink from your river of delights.

– **PSALM 36:8** –

Jesus said He intends to fill us with His joy. *Fill.* Not just a wave of joy here and there, an hour or so of God-bequeathed happiness once a week, a drop or two on a cloudy day. No, He wants to fill us with joy. Our joy will *overflow*, He said.

In a women's Bible study group, we were talking about Jesus' words on joy found in John 14 and 15. Someone suggested that there are buckets and barrels of joy available.

And then one woman spoke up. "But we just go to God with our little teaspoons."

Yes, that describes me, I thought. God says He will supply an overwhelming abundance of gifts and mercies; but I arrive at His throne with just a teaspoon.

After that day (with my little teaspoon still in hand), I started noticing big words in Scripture. *Big* as in *holding great proportions.*

When God tells us what He has for His children, He uses words of enormous and unlimited proportions. That is His loving character and kindness—enormous and unlimited.

Here's a sampling of the words I found. Many

of these passages we can rattle off by memory and it's tempting just to skim right over them, but STOP!

Then proceed slowly. Hear the extravagance, completeness, and perfection conveyed by the words I've put in italics.

All of this, God promises, is available to His children. Listen to the language:*

you will be *filled* with my joy. Yes, your joy will *overflow!*

hope will not lead to disappointment, because we know how *dearly* God loves us

may the God of hope *fill* you with *all* joy and peace... so that you may *overflow* with hope...

the God who gives *life to the dead* and *creates new things out of nothing*

the earth is *filled* with your love, O Lord

to know this love that *surpasses* knowledge

you will experience God's peace, which *exceeds* anything we can understand

he who began a good work in you will carry it on to *completion*

grace and peace be yours in *abundance*

with God *all* things are *possible*

him who is able to do *immeasurably more* than all we ask or imagine

rebirth and renewal by the Holy Spirit whom he *poured* out on us *generously*

this *all-surpassing* power is from God

out of his *glorious riches* he may strengthen you with power

His *divine power* has given us *everything* we need for life and godliness

He is able, once and *forever*, to save those who come to God through him

ask God, who gives *generously* to all

though your sins are like scarlet, they shall be as *white as snow*

as far as the east is from the west, so far has he removed our transgressions from us

and this is what he promised us - even *eternal* life

and my God will meet *all* your needs according to his *glorious* riches

I am come that they may have life, and have it *to the full*

God's *abundant* provision of grace... brings life for all men

how *priceless* is your *unfailing* love!

they feast on the *abundance* of your house

the Lord's *unfailing* love *surrounds* the man who trusts in him

his *incomparably great* power for us who believe

Did you catch the full weight of all those words in italics? God apparently does not deal in drops or smidges or smatterings or pinches or trickles or dabs or teaspoons. Not even in buckets and barrels. He pours and fills to overflowing; He promises and is faithful and unfailing; and He completes and perfects.

God's vocabulary of abundance saturates Scripture. What if we start looking for the hugeness of His promises, start thinking in His dimensions, and start believing and living in God proportions?

That's impossible, of course. As long as we dwell in these human tents, we can never fully understand the deep reservoirs of God. But we can ask the Spirit for a glimpse! We can ask Him to start pouring into us all the richness He can give His children.

Our Psalm prayer for this section asks for just that—that God will show us this abundance of life He's given us.

Then we can begin to believe-live a life in heavenly realities. We will toss out the teaspoons.

And we'll sit down to enjoy the feast—even in the presence of our enemies.

* Taken from various translations: John 15:11, Romans 5:5, Romans 15:13, Romans 4:17, Psalm 119:64, Ephesians 3:19, Philippians 4:7, Philippians 1:6, 1 Peter 1:2, Matthew 19:26, Ephesians 3:20, Titus 3:5, 6, 2 Corinthians 4:7, Ephesians 3:16, 2 Peter 1:3, Hebrews 7:25, James 1:5, Isaiah 1:18, Psalm 103:12, 1 John 2:25, Philippians 4:19, John 10:10, Romans 5:17, Psalm 36:7, Psalm 36:8, Psalm 32:10, Ephesians 1:19.

ᗟᘐᗷ MANY WONDERS FOR US ᗷᘐᗟ

*So don't be afraid, little flock. For it gives your Father
great happiness to give you the Kingdom.*

– **LUKE 12:32** –

I'm often fascinated by the unpredictability of our memory. We forget things we might reasonably expect to remember. And then there are simple, seemingly insignificant moments that stay with us for a lifetime.

One of those "small" moments that I've never forgotten occurred over thirty years ago. I was coming home after a weekend away. I expected to open the door to a cold, dark apartment; but instead, there was a cheerful fire burning in the fireplace and fresh flowers on the table.

Aha. Mom and Dad have been here. I knew immediately.

That was my mom and dad. They modeled for me a giving that went beyond duty. If I asked Dad to do A, he would often notice that B also needed some attention and he'd go ahead and do that, too. Mom and Dad both would go out of their way to be kind and thoughtful and give whatever they had to give whenever they had opportunity.

I learned from their example that there is joy in giving abundantly, above and beyond the minimum effort or input required.

Maybe you're a parent and know the joy of being able to give your children not only what they need but beyond—giving gifts that enrich their lives. Or it may be in other types of relationships that you have taken joy in giving gifts that add happiness and enjoyment to a loved one's life.

Our hope knows that our heavenly Father also takes joy in giving to His children—except that He operates on a much grander scale than we humans ever achieve. Our hope trusts that He is the source of all good gifts; He delights in doing great things for His people; and for us, He is the source of everything that is the "good life."

I believe He delights in doing what we would call the "small" things for us, too, those small gifts that come into our lives every day and bring us happiness. We might call them *coincidences.* I don't agree. I believe they are God's hand, the heavenly Father personally touching that hour of our day.

The book of Psalms is full of joy. (I guess I've already mentioned that, haven't I?) On almost every page, you'll find a reference to life, joy, happiness, gladness, or rejoicing—right alongside the laments about suffering, hard battles, and emotional valleys. The songwriters often outlined their reasons for rejoicing.

Because He dearly loves His children, the

Holy God of the universe:

- heals our diseases
- clears our record of guilt
- defeats our enemies and arms us with His weapons and strength
- leads beside still waters and satisfies desires with good things
- hides us in times of trouble, guides with His counsel
- and holds us safe as we walk through fire and flood

And that's only the beginning of the list. This sums it up:

> *O LORD my God, you have performed many wonders for us. Your plans for us are too numerous to list. You have no equal. If I tried to recite all your wonderful deeds, I would never come to the end of them.* (Psalm 40:5)

I wonder: if you tried to recite all God has done for you, what sort of things would your memory bring back? The big things and the small things, life-changing things and the simple, good gifts He pours out every day. Is your memory full of it all?

To be honest, I hesitated as I wrote this meditation. Might it sound as though we're in this relationship with the heavenly Father because of what *we* get out of it? And yet, this is all true. Our attempts and solutions and schemes always fall short. The ultimate answers are always found in our relationship with Him, and He does all this for us because He loves us.

This is what hope knows: The Lord delights in blessing His children, and He supplies everything we need for living life to the fullest. That's the subject of this entire book.

The opening verse from the Gospel of Luke was spoken by Jesus, as He talked to His disciples about worries and concerns over money, possessions, and basic needs. I hear great tenderness in His words as He said, *Don't be afraid, little flock.* The Father not only supplies what we need, but He goes beyond and is pleased to give us everything we've inherited as His children, heirs to the Kingdom!

FULLNESS OF LIFE AND POWER

May you experience the love of Christ, though it is too great to understand fully. Then you will be made complete with all the fullness of life and power that comes from God.
– **EPHESIANS 3:19** –

Let's push one step further toward this full and satisfying life, a life of abundance beyond our imagining. That's what we want, isn't it?

There is one verse about joy—complete joy—that we have not yet touched. And as I wrote this section, I found myself trying to move this verse to the background. I wasn't ready to tackle everything it means, everything it demands. There is that constant war between my old self, with its allegiance only to me, and my new self, with allegiance to the Spirit of Christ.

I think I've already alerted you to the fact that I don't have all the answers. I am still on the path of learning how to live as a child of God and with great expectation. So my confession now will not surprise you.

My old self doesn't want to think about this verse because it shoves me toward change and growth—and I'm pretty sure the learning will sometimes be painful. It seems so much easier and more comfortable to sit in my old habits and complacency.

Among the Scriptures that spoke to me of a *full, rich life,* I found one that I couldn't forget or ignore. Opening my mind and heart to this truth has been hard, so bear with me as I try to explain the ongoing battle between the old selfish me and the new me that wants to throw myself into the arms of the Spirit and live fully in lavish abundance.

I apologize in advance if the following pages are confusing and difficult to follow. If it makes you dizzy to try to follow my thoughts, skip it and get on to the next section.

The opening Scripture (Ephesians 3:19) refers to being made complete with all the fullness of life and power that comes from God.

Can you imagine? What would it be like to live with all the fullness of life and power God can give? I can only guess that it is like God's incredible power—far beyond anything our minds can grasp. And equally amazing is the implication that we can have that kind of life right now, while we are still on the human pilgrimage, while we are still imperfect.

Even though I can't imagine what that life would be like, I know it is exactly the life I want!

Look at the context of this hope and promise in Ephesians 3. Notice the progression: First, the Spirit starts imbuing my life with His strength. Christ makes His home with me and I learn to trust Him. My roots go down deeper and deeper into God's love and I'm kept strong.

And I start to understand Christ's amazing love for me. Even though it's so great that I'll never understand fully, I start to see the depth, the vast proportions, and the reach of it.

And when I *experience* the love of Christ, then I will be made complete with all the fullness of life and power that comes from God.

So, this full, abundant, overflowing life and power is all tied up with *experiencing* Christ's love.

When Paul spoke of *experiencing* the love of Christ, I believe He was talking about much more than just *receiving* Christ's love for myself.

When we experience a bond of love between two people, it is not only one person who is loved and one who is giving love. Both are giving and receiving. That is experiencing love.

In the same way, it's my belief that when Paul wrote of experiencing the love of Christ, he was talking about much more than realizing how much Christ loves me. Paul was also talking about the love of Christ flowing out of me. *That* is the experience of Christ's love—to know it activated within me!

And when that happens—when Christ's love operates in us—we are made "complete with all the fullness of life and power from God."

That completeness and fullness of life and power are somehow all wrapped up with Christ's love operating out of our lives.

Uh-oh.

This brings me back to the passage I've been avoiding: John 15:9-12.

That passage is part of Jesus' farewell words to His disciples. He told them, "I've told you all these things so you will be filled with overflowing joy. My joy." And the key to having this overflowing joy is in obeying His commandment: "Love each other in the same way I have loved you."

There's the rub.

I want the complete, powerful, and full life. I want the overflowing joy. But too often, I just don't want to love like Jesus loves. That is, the old me doesn't want to.

Because loving others as Jesus loves is hard. I will have to learn a lot about loving, and I'm pretty sure God will have to prune me quite a bit.

It's easier to stay in my own kingdom and live the way I want, rather than live under this guiding rule of the Kingdom of Heaven.

But... I don't want to live in my own kingdom, according to my own rules. That never ends well.

I am reluctant. Okay, I'm afraid. I am afraid to acquiesce and say to the Spirit, "Make me over completely. Teach me how to love like you do."

But why be afraid? We've been promised that living according to the Spirit brings life and peace. The fruit of the Spirit includes love, joy, and peace.

Ah. Those things I so desire are all wrapped up together, intertwined, interdependent. All of those can come into my life because the Spirit has the power to rewire me.

I know it will take that power of the Spirit to remake me, because this is something I can't do on my own. I've already confessed my resistance, and that reluctance to learn to love is standing in the way of my experiencing this fullness of life and power from God.

You see how the battle goes on within me?

I know where my allegiance, my love, and my longings lie. Love, joy, peace. *All* the fullness of life and power from God. That is what I want.

So I take great comfort reading further in Ephesians 3—and finding that God can do things in me that I can't even imagine.

My hope is counting on that.

And I also depend on 2 Corinthians 3:17-18 that assures me the Spirit is daily changing me, making me more and more like Christ.

So that I will learn to love like Jesus loves, and my reluctance and selfishness will be overcome by His love for others, burning in me.

And I will begin to experience that *ultimate* fullness of life and power and joy and peace.

For more words on God's abundant goodness for our lives,
see the appendix for a list of additional Scriptures.

PRAYER IN THE HARD PLACES:

O God, give me comfort in my suffering. Renew my life by your promise.

– Adapted from **PSALM 119:50** –

GOOD THINGS OUT OF HARD PLACES

✦✦ GOD IN THE WILDERNESS ✦✦

For the L<small>ORD</small> *your God is bringing you into a good land...*

– **DEUTERONOMY 8:7** –

There's yet another gap in the last section. We focused on joy, but I omitted numerous verses about "great joy." If we're going to contemplate *abundant and satisfying life,* wouldn't you think I'd include all the references I could find about *great joy?*

For example, James 1:2 says that when we

meet trouble, we have an opportunity for great joy. Peter wrote that there is wonderful joy ahead, even though now we are in terrible suffering. And Jesus said we can be happy and leap for joy when people hate and mock and curse us.

You see the puzzling contradiction. It seems that the greatest joy will come out of the greatest pain and trouble.

And so, although we're going to talk about hard places and pain and persecution, I chose to open this section with the declaration that *the* LORD *your God is bringing you into a good land!*

This section of meditations has been difficult to write. For one thing, every heart knows its own pain, but I have no idea what suffering you are going through. I understand the suffering that I've walked through in my own life, and I can identify with those of you going through similar hard times. But there is so much trouble in the world that I know nothing of. The fire you are now walking through is probably quite different from the flood that threatens me.

Yet I believe in God's promises to all His children. And every one of us, in any culture or time of life, needs this bridge of hope to take us forward: the promise that God brings good things out of hard places.

We do not hold that hope simply because

we like to be optimistic. Oh my, no. Even the most cheerful optimist can be staggered by great tragedy, suffering, or persecution. Nothing in the following pages is intended to make light of the hard times we must go through. The opening quote from Moses, in its context in Deuteronomy, was preceded by *forty years' time* of wandering and suffering in a wilderness. We know full well that hard times come to everyone's life.

Rather than simply trying to be optimistic, we hold this hope for another reason: We believe that what God says is truth. Our hope knows.

Entire libraries have been written on pain and suffering; we're only going to take a few pages here. But we'll get a glimpse of this great hope we have as children of God, because our hope has heard the promise that no matter what storms are battering our ships, God is working in the storm.

Or, to use another metaphor: No matter what wilderness you're struggling through, God is bringing you into a good land.

༈ FEASTS IN THE PRESENCE ༈
OF ENEMIES

Dear brothers and sisters, when troubles come your way,
consider it an opportunity for great joy.
- JAMES 1:2 -

They were being thrown to the lions.
Literally. Ostracized from their former comfort
zones. Having to meet and celebrate in secret.
Hunted down and arrested. Then beheaded or
thrown into the arena so that an audience could
be entertained by the spectacle of their deaths.
Christians in the first century knew hard times.

How could James have the audacity to write
a letter to these people and say, *This is your
opportunity for great joy?* It was not only James
who wrote this kind of assurance; throughout the
early Christian letters in the New Testament, we
find many expressions of encouragement to stand
strong, endure the hard times, and know that God
will still work His plan through it all.

How could they write such assurances? We
read the next line for the answer: Because you
know that trials help you develop perseverance.
And persevering through it all brings you to a
place of maturity and perfection! (James 1:3-4)

How did they know good things would come
out of these terrible situations? When our lives

take unexpected, painful twists, how can we still have hope? How can we hold hope even while we're suffering physically or our hearts are breaking?

During the days I was working on this section, there were two tragedies in my small corner of the world. Two huge upheavals brought death and changed many lives. The people who were affected were constantly on my mind. As I witnessed the breaking apart of their lives, I could not hide in clichés or offer panaceas or glib recitals of Scripture.

But as my heart ached for these people, I heard Jesus saying in the storm to scared-to-death disciples, "I am here" (Matthew 14:27).

I hear Him also say those words to me and to anyone in the midst of life-shaking turmoil.

I hear Him say that He is the Great Shepherd of our souls.

I go back to that psalm of comfort, Psalm 23, that assures the flock that the Shepherd supplies everything we need. And there is the line that even when we are surrounded by our enemies, the Shepherd prepares us feasts, anoints us with healing, and pours out blessings until our cup cannot hold them all.

When we are in a hard place, it's difficult to taste the feast. When we are completely drained and exhausted, the overflowing cup of blessings might seem like a foolish dream. When our wounds are raw and gushing blood and life itself seems to be draining away, then healing feels impossible and "perfection and maturity" seem to be demanding too high a price.

But the Great Shepherd of our souls died to give us this life. And in the middle of everything that seems to work against us, He is still shepherding us, still providing for us, and yes, even pouring out blessings of heaven.

Hope knows this, and we stake our lives on this Way, this Truth, and this Life.

❦ HE GOES BEFORE US ❦

And we know that God causes everything to work together for the good of those who love God and are called according to his purpose for them.
— ROMANS 8:28 —

Their youngest son went for a walk one day and never came back. The only thing that was found was a piece of clothing belonging to the boy—smeared with blood.

Can you imagine a harder place? The boy's parents had no clue as to what had happened to their child, but that bloody coat indicated violence. Yet a body was never found, nor was a perpetrator of the crime ever suspected, accused, or punished. They spent many years grieving and wondering.

And I'm sure the father, especially, had many questions for God. His life up to that point had been anything but peaceful. There had been so much turmoil. He knew and believed God's promises, but his path had been through many hard times. He had been battered by so many storms. Had he not suffered enough? Why had God allowed this to happen now? This was too much to bear. It was such a staggering blow that he lived his life in constant and deep mourning. Can you imagine the prayers, the tears, the questions, the heavy sadness that would not lift?

Recently, I read the account again, and I wept when I came to the ending. I knew how the story turned out, because this is the story of Joseph and his father, Jacob. We've known this story since we were children. Yet reading it this time, I was touched like never before.

I wept not in sadness, but in relief and thankfulness.

You know the end of the story. Jacob discovered that God had had a hand in his life all along. At their reunion, Jacob's once-lost son said, "God has gone ahead of us, setting the stage so that I can save us all now."

But oh! the hard places Jacob, the bereaved father, had to walk through!

There are so many Scriptures that tell us that God holds the lives of His children. He not only walks through everything with us (remember Jesus' words, *Take courage. I am here*), but He has a plan and He uses everything that happens to achieve His plan.

Several years ago, I joined a small group who decided to read the Bible through in four months, reading the Scriptures in chronological order. (Let me, right now, recommend this to you. Benefits and blessings will come that you cannot imagine.) Reading the Bible through in this way makes so many things clear: God has a plan for His creation. He is in control and carrying out His plan. And He has a plan for each one of us, too, and is carrying that out also.

But in the hard places, we hurt and cry and struggle and rage. And we need those bridges of hope that we can trust to take us forward.

I want to pull out just two passages today that always speak peace to me. They're taken from contrasting situations. The first is written to people who are in the middle of terrifying opposition and great suffering. The second addresses a people on the verge of a wonderful new life.

Trust your lives to the God who created you, for he will never fail you. (1 Peter 4:19)

For the Lord your God is bringing you into a good land of flowing streams and pools of water... a land where food is plentiful and nothing is lacking. (Deuteronomy 8:7,9)

Our hope knows that in the good times and in the most terrifying times, our lives are safe in His hands because He has a plan for us and He is bringing us, even through the wilderness, to the good place He promised.

Our sight and comprehension are so limited. Especially in the hard places of our journeys, we find it difficult to see what God is doing. Yet we have that promise in Romans 8:28. We recite it glibly, and it's been used so much and in so many ways that I fear it has lost its impact. And I'm guessing that most of us have, at one time or another, questioned this verse. We've said, "What good can possibly come out of this?"

But an absolute trust and belief in this promise can change our lives.

We may not be able to see or understand what God is doing in the moment, but if we stand firmly on this bridge of hope, then we *know* that even in the most terrible and terrifying parts of our journey, God is there, already ahead of us, working to bring good things out of those hard places.

ᨄᨄ PAIN, GAIN: GOD'S GRACE ᨄᨄ FOR HIS CHILDREN

My purpose in writing is to encourage you and assure you that what you are experiencing is truly part of God's grace for you. Stand firm in this grace.

— from **1 PETER 5:12** —

How would you feel if you were struggling through a hard place and you received a letter with the above lines? I might be tempted to tear it up in anger.

This is part of God's grace for you. Who wants to hear such words in the middle of tough, painful times?

But wait, child of God. The tough times we walk through—whether you want to name it fire, flood, terrifying wilderness, or Valley of Weeping—are all bathed in God's grace.

What does that mean?

This is the shining hope of the Scriptures from the beginning, when God chose a people as His own, to the revelations of the future: The heavenly Father disciplines everyone He loves, so that we grow up with the strong and godly character He means for His children to have.

And there's that word: discipline.

Can we somehow separate the word *discipline* from the controversies surrounding it in today's society? *Discipline* has been tainted by the abuse of authority, by the violence we've seen, particularly against children, by the substitution of punishment and power, and by worldly entities trying to dictate what is right and wrong in raising children.

Shed all the emotional connotations that have stuck to the word, and go to its definition. *Discipline* is training, forming, instruction, and exercise. It's cutting out what has to go, and toughening and strengthening what we desire to increase.

I'm sure you've seen the phrase on athletes' shirts: "No pain, no gain." We have no trouble accepting that statement as truth for the athlete's life. Athletes proclaim it proudly and live it passionately. Yet when we apply the same principle to our spiritual lives, we shrink back, much preferring that it would be "No pain, abundant gain!"

But just as that does not work in the training of an athlete, it does not work in our faith training.

Parents concerned about forming the

character of their child will use daily life—the pleasant and the painful—as the classroom to instruct and guide their children. Our heavenly Father does the same, using tests and trials, from the little, day-to-day irritations to life-threatening persecutions. He uses it all to teach us and build endurance, faith, patience, and godliness in us, forming our character.

That is the working of His grace for us. His kindness bestows good things, even in and out of the hard places.

And so, would you think me crazy for rejoicing when I walk through a terrifying wilderness? Hope watches and waits for the manna of grace in the wilderness.

It is this hope that I hold as my church denomination goes through a purifying fire. Yet God's grace is working—I see it in the church family and in individuals as good things unexpectedly come out of the sad and painful situation. I hold this hope for myself as I tell Jesus I want to love as He loves, but I know the training for such great love will include pain and hard places. Yet how else will I learn? How else does the heart expand with new space to love? Pain, gain. Discipline, training, growing up in godliness.

Even Jesus learned obedience through

suffering (Hebrews 5:8). When we talk of the "suffering" of Christ, we think of Him hanging on a cross—but have you ever read the Gospels and thought about the suffering He lived through every day?

Hear the loneliness in His words, "Foxes have holes, but I have nowhere to lay my head."

His closest friends often did not understand His purpose and message.

Remember the tears He shed over a city that stubbornly refused to hear His message?

Think about what it must have been like to be rejected by the religious establishment, that entity around which all of Jewish life revolved. He never had a comfortable position in the "in" circles. Even in His family circle, there was the suspicion that Jesus was mentally ill.

When He went back home to visit, the gossip started... you know how that goes. The crowd worked themselves into such rage that they even tried to kill Him—His former friends and neighbors!

And that final night in Gethsemane when He knew what lay ahead—did He have any idea of the brutality He would endure even before His body was nailed to a cross? As He stood before Pilate, bloody and beaten, do you think the human part of Him was tempted to just give it up and abandon the mission? He could have been out of the whole mess with just a wave of His hand.

He *suffered* as He followed through with God's plan for His life.

And so I keep my eyes on my big brother, my example, who came to show me what living in the kingdom of light is all about, and I want to grow up to be like Him.

Oswald Chambers wrote in *My Utmost for His Highest:*

> *Thank God that He does give us difficult things to do! His salvation is a joyous thing, but it is also something that requires bravery, courage, and holiness. It tests us for all we are worth. Jesus is "bringing many sons to glory" (Hebrews 2:10), and God will not shield us from the requirements of sonship. God's grace produces men and women with a strong family likeness to Jesus Christ, not pampered, spoiled weaklings.*

I don't want to be a pampered, spoiled weakling. I want the family likeness to be seen in me.

For too much of my life, I've just run away from hard times and looked for safe places to hide. But I am now more afraid of staying in those seeming "safe" places than I am of having to walk through the wilderness or the Valley of Weeping. It is in the places of complacency and self-assured security that we are in great danger of being gulped down by the roaring lion who is prowling about, our enemy, the devil.

I don't want that!

I much prefer the wilderness, even with its desert and poisonous snakes and scorpions— where God's grace will train me and grow strength and endurance and godliness in me.

OUR EYES SEE HIM

The LORD of Heaven's Armies is here among us;
He is our fortress.

– PSALM 46:11 –

Even though I'm a reader thousands of years away from the story of Job, I still have to ask the Lord, *Why? Why would you allow all this trouble to fall on one man's head?*

But I read the end of the story, and I find, not the answer to *Why,* but an amazing thing that blazes a desire in my own heart.

Go back to the beginning of the account. Meet Job. He lived an upright life. He was blameless, had complete integrity, and stayed away from evil. God called him "my servant." Yet hear what

Job says after all his suffering:

"I had only heard about you before, but now I have seen you with my own eyes." (Job 42:5)

For Job, the hard times included loss of property, family, and health; anger; questioning; and friends who didn't understand and doubted Job's integrity. Yet the experience had brought Job a more personal relationship with God than he had ever known before.

In our trials and troubles, God opens the door to draw us closer, teach us more, and show us more of Himself.

We can, of course, be angry with Him and turn away and refuse to see Him. Or we could be too ashamed, knowing we are in deep trouble because of our own unwise choices. We might try to hide from God for a time.

But when we look, when we open our eyes, we will see that He is here with us, in the middle of the mess.

Psalm 46 is the song that starts out with earthquakes and mountains crumbling and tidal waves roaring. That could be natural disasters or it might be our private worlds suffering such great devastation.

Yet we will not fear, the song declares. Nations might be in chaos and kingdoms crumbling. The earth might even be melting! But the place of God's presence is secure.

> *God dwells in that city; it cannot be destroyed. From the very break of day, God will protect it. The LORD of Heaven's Armies is here among us; [He] is our fortress.* (Psalm 46:5, 11)

Remember that God now dwells among His people. We are His Temple here on earth. He makes His home with us; His presence is here. In the midst of chaos and crumbling and disaster and yes, even our guilt, we, like Job, will see Him with our own eyes if we seek Him.

That's part of His kindness for us in the hard places. He is always right there, with us.

It's a security we can depend on.

WORDS OF HOPE, BRIDGES TO TAKE US ONWARD

Your promise revives me;
it comforts me in all my troubles.
— **PSALM 119:50** —

If hard times and struggles create a training ground for us, what can we gain by our pain? When we go through dark days without a ray of light; when we lie awake at night because the mind will not rest; when we look everywhere and cannot find relief or answers or help; when we bleed and break and cry—yet still, the children of God have this hope: God does bring good things out of even the most terrifying wilderness.

For every child of God going through a hard time, there's hope in Scripture, laid out in plain words and speaking directly to your soul. Here's just a beginning list, with some of my comments:

James 1:2. Testing produces perseverance in us. And perseverance will make us "perfect and complete." I know I'm far from that point of completeness. I also know I want it. Shall I welcome testing?

1 Peter 1:6-7. When your faith remains strong through testing, it will bring you "much praise and honor" when Jesus Christ and His heavenly kingdom appear.

Psalm 66:8-12. God purifies us in hard times, and He brings us through fire and flood, to a "place of great abundance." I want purification. I want to know that place of abundance. I want to live there.

2 Corinthians 6:10. We have spiritual riches and joy in spite of heartache.

Deuteronomy 8:2-3, 11-18. We learn humility. We learn that it is God and God alone who brings us through the wilderness to a place of abundance.

We learn to depend on Him instead of being too proud of our own resources.

Romans 5:3-4. Problems and trials help us develop endurance which in turn creates godly character in us and increases our trust and hope in God.

2 Corinthians 12:9-10 and Hebrews 2:18. We have a greater experience of Christ's presence, power, and help.

Daniel 11:35. Persecution refines us. Purifies us. Even cleanses us.

Psalm 31:7-8. God cares about our anguish, our suffering opens us to see His unfailing love, and through it all, He keeps us in a safe place.

Matthew 5:4 and Isaiah 61:3. His comfort comes to those who mourn.

2 Thessalonians 3:2-3. He strengthens us and guards us.

Hebrews 10:12-13 and Romans 8:28. God uses everything that happens to develop godliness in us and use us according to His purposes.

1 Peter 5:10. God does not abandon us in our hard times. He will restore, support, and strengthen us and put our feet on solid ground once again.

That last verse from Peter is one of my favorites. It spoke to me during a time in my life when everything seemed to be changing—and not for the better. I longed for that promised "solid ground" because it seemed there was nothing I could depend on. That verse and the hope it held became a bridge laid before me, enabling me to keep going forward even when I didn't know how going forward would be possible.

May you find your bridges of hope, too.

✧✦✧ REAPING JOY FROM TEARS ✧✦✧

No discipline is enjoyable while it is happening—it's painful! But afterward there will be a peaceful harvest of right living for those who are trained in this way.

– HEBREWS 12:11 –

In our sorrows and pain, are seeds being planted that will bring harvests of joy? Can we hold that hope?

Psalm 126:5-6 creates that picture. People who had been exiled from their homeland returned to a devastated land and wanted to rebuild their lives. They walked in grief and tears, but they planted in hope and looked forward to a harvest of joy.

What might the harvest be of our own grief and tears?

I think we will be harvesting in the Lord's fields.

In "making all things work together" for His

purposes, the Almighty Father uses our hard times to bring good harvests in the lives of others, too.

Recall the scene described in Acts 2. The Holy Spirit filled the disciples, and they began speaking to crowds gathered in Jerusalem for Pentecost. The disciples were speaking in languages they had not known before. Those people from out of town looked at each other in amazement, saying, "This person speaks our language. And he's talking about wonderful things God has done!"

While we're trudging through the wilderness, we usually cannot see what wonderful things God has planned to bring out of our suffering, but one thing I have experienced and do know: Out of our hard times comes a new language, a language we can now speak to others who are traveling through the same barren wilderness.

Who better to speak to the grief of a lonely widow than another widow who has also walked through that valley? Who knows better the power of Christ to free from addiction than a person whom Christ has freed? Who better to speak the language of the hard times of divorce than one who has had to walk through that fire? Who knows the language of depression better than those who live with it?

When Paul writes about the gifts given to the church to carry out their ministry in the world, might suffering also be a gift? Can God use my trials and troubles to carry hope and comfort to another person who is experiencing the same thing I've been through?

> *God is our merciful Father and the source of all comfort. He comforts us in all our troubles so that we can comfort others. When they are troubled, we will be able to give them the same comfort God has given us. For the more we suffer for Christ, the more God will shower us with his comfort through Christ.* (2 Corinthians 1:3-5)

There is so much hope in this passage. God is the source of all comfort. Not only does He comfort us, but He comforts others through us.

I'd like to introduce you to Vaneetha Rendall, whom I met a few years ago in an online writing group. Vaneetha has walked through valleys I have not walked; she has lost a child, a husband, and her health. She can speak languages I cannot. Here are some of her words. "Paul" is the son she lost.

> *In sharing about Paul and subsequent sorrows, I have found others desperate for words of hope and comfort. They want to talk about their pain and fears with someone who has suffered as they have. It has been an honor to be part of their healing. To listen to them as they*

*walk similar paths of sorrow. To offer
evidence that they will heal, survive and
even thrive. I hear others asking the same
questions I did: Will I make it through?
Will the aching ever stop? Will I ever
laugh again?*

*God has carried me in my grief and
comforted me through terrible trials. And
because of His tender care, I am able to
offer hope to others who are suffering.
And when I do, it is like rubbing balm on
my wounds. I get stronger. I gain courage.
I feel joy again.*

You can read more of Vaneetha's story and
words of hope at her website, *danceintherain.com*
or on *www.desiringgod.org/vaneetha.*

Isn't this amazing grace?

God brings good things from our hard places,
not only for us, but also for the benefit of others.
The gifts that are given to God's children include
the gift of the language of suffering. In those
languages, we can speak hope to each other.

God works in our pain so that, *with joy,* we
can be part of others' healing. And as we do, we
grow stronger, gain more courage, and feel joy
again.

Plant in tears. Reap in joy.

This same idea of *harvest* is found in the

Hebrews passage that opens this meditation. We usually read that verse with our own suffering in mind, looking for encouragement to endure. Yet, read it again, thinking of how God might be training us to be sowing and reaping joy in *other* lives.

Yes, I believe that our suffering trains us to be better partners with Jesus. God is shaping and molding us not only for the sake of our own holiness; He is also training us to be more effective in Jesus' ongoing work in this world. Jesus suffered for us. We have joined Him in His mission to this world. Should our training be any less than His? Will we endure our suffering so that we can serve God by traveling with others through their wilderness?

PERSECUTION: OPPORTUNITIES, PRIVILEGES, REWARDS

That is why we never give up. Though our bodies are dying, our spirits are being renewed every day. For our present troubles are small and won't last very long. Yet they produce for us a glory that vastly outweighs them and will last forever.

– **2 CORINTHIANS 4:16-17** –

How's that for a title? Does it sound like a slick sales spiel prompting you to sign up for something you don't really want?

Let me say right here that I know very little of the language of persecution. But I believe I'm going to have to learn it soon. North American Christians are facing more and more opposition to their faith and living their faith. The hostility and antagonism toward Christ followers is growing stronger and more widespread. So although I cannot speak much from experience, I want to prepare myself. I want the Spirit to be forming my thinking now concerning what lies ahead.

Of course, the earthly life in me says, *Hold on a minute!* and shrinks back at the prospect of being the target of hate and trouble because I carry the name of Christ. Yet the new, heavenly life within me has set my heart on something more than my own comfort: the opportunities, privileges, and rewards that come through persecution because I am connected to Christ.

Yes, the hope we are given is that these things will come to those who are persecuted because they follow Jesus.

OPPORTUNITY

We have words about the opportunities of persecution from Jesus Himself. First, He does not sugarcoat the facts of the life He calls us to. He doesn't have a promo that promises all glory and blessing. He tells us bluntly that those who are His disciples will encounter all kinds of trouble.

But this is an opportunity! He says. On a worldly level, it is a hard life He is calling us to; but in His kingdom, in the values and dynamics of heaven, this is opportunity!

In Luke 21, Jesus talked to His disciples about the future and His eventual return to the earth. And He assured them that hard times were—*are*—ahead. His followers would be dragged before courts and thrown in jail. They would actually be on trial. We could make all those sentences present tense, happening now.

Jesus added, "But this will be your opportunity to tell them about me" (Luke 21:13).

Jesus' focus is on spreading the Gospel. He reminds us that our short breath of life is but part of a much larger picture, one that is centered on God's will for His creation. And His will for His children is that we become a part of His work here on this earth, bearers of the message that God wants people to come back to Him and He's made a way for us to do so.

In 2 Corinthians 4, Paul writes about hard times (including persecution), and reminds us that our steadfastness in these times can show Christ's life shining through ours. It's a chance to show God's power and faithfulness to His people. Our standing firm is an opportunity to spread the word to more and more people about God's love and kindness.

God has a plan, you see, and His children are partners with the Rescuer Christ Jesus in carrying out the plan. We are called to do good and spread the Gospel, even if it means suffering, just as Christ suffered so that we could become God's children. He is our example. We follow in His steps (see 1 Peter 2:21).

PRIVILEGE

And that is the great privilege—to be partners with Christ in His rescue work. To bear His name.

I'm thinking of how proudly some wear jerseys with the names or numbers of their favorite football players. Or tee shirts with business names. In the book of Acts, we find the disciples flogged for the preaching they've been doing; and when they're released, they rejoiced that God had "counted them worthy to bear disgrace for the name of Jesus."

In our suffering for the sake of furthering the Gospel mission, we become partners with Christ. And the wonderful thing about that partnership is that He is there, helping us. Because He went through trials and suffering Himself, He helps us now (see Hebrews 2:18). When we're under attack from the world, we know it also attacked Him. We're partners.

And as His partners, we have His Spirit and power working through us. Our lives are so closely connected to Him that we are like vine and branches. Our weakness makes room for His great power. After a stroke that affected his vision and writing, Steve Fuller wrote, "Every trial is a gift of more of Christ's presence."

Christ pours Himself into us.

Becoming a part and a partner of Christ— what a privilege!

I want to be worthy of wearing His name and of being His partner in this mission.

REWARD

"Dance for joy," Jesus said, "when people hate you because you follow me. How God will bless you now and in the future! And a great reward awaits you in heaven." (See Luke 6:22-23 and Matthew 5:11-12).

That situation sounds familiar—people hating and mocking and cursing you because you follow Jesus. We see and hear that every day.

If this happens to you, says Jesus, you have a great reward awaiting you. And as we listen to His words and read the rest of God's promises, we know that this reward is going to be exciting!

For now, those few words of Jesus are enough to plant my feet firmly and point my eyes ahead to a new life in the new city.

And maybe I'll dance for joy now, even in the hard places.

᠊ᠰᠠᠠᠠᡵ CONFIDENT HOPE ᠆ᠠᠠᠠᠠᡵ

I am coming soon. Hold on to what you have.

– Jesus, in REVELATION 3:11 –

This has been a long section. Yet it seems we've only begun to grasp the deep hope we have even when we go through hard times. None of us can avoid the rough and dangerous roads in our journeys. But God, true to His promises, is there to help us and bring good out of even the painful, destructive, and evil.

May I squeeze in a few more words?

I am compelled to include a second quote from Oswald Chambers in *My Utmost for His Highest* because it describes so well how I feel at times and also voices my hope for those hard times.

A saint's life is in the hands of God like a bow and arrow in the hands of an archer. God is aiming at something the saint cannot see, but our LORD continues to stretch and strain, and every once in a while the saint says, "I can't take any more." Yet God pays no attention; He goes on stretching until His purpose is in sight, and then He lets the arrow fly. Entrust yourself to God's hands.

Peace to you, brothers and sisters, trusting yourself to the God who created you and gave you this life. He will never abandon you.

No matter what hard time you're going through,

Rejoice in our confident hope. Be patient in trouble, and keep on praying. (Romans 12:12)

For more promises as you go through hard times, see the appendix for a list of additional Scriptures.

PRAYER FOR WEARY SOULS:

I earnestly search for you. My soul thirsts for you in this parched and weary land where there is no water.

\- **from PSALM 63:1** \-

REFRESHMENT FOR
THE WEARY

"HE RESTORETH MY SOUL"

For you are the fountain of life...
- PSALM 36:9 -

When we are tired. When the questions are so hard and there are still no answers. When there are only dark clouds and no rainbow shines through the rain. When the bills are endless and the boss is unreasonable and our family drives us crazy. When we've been harshly criticized for doing what we thought was right. When we just can't feel God in our day.

What then?

Where do we go? What lifesaving line do we grab and hold onto?

You recognize the title above, straight from that beloved psalm we've referred to again and again. We all know times when we cry out to God that we need to have restoration of our souls.

In this psalm about the Great Shepherd who provides everything His people need, these four words are tucked into a picture of peace and refreshment. Different translations of the Bible use slightly different words:

He restoreth my soul.

He renews my strength.

He refreshes my soul.

He renews my life.

He revives my life.

All translations, to my mind, claim the same hope: He gives refreshment in parched places. As we come through those hard places, we can confidently expect that God, in His great kindness to His children, will bring us times of healing, nourishment, and rest.

If you remember the opening verse in the last section, it assured us that God is bringing us into a good land. And when we look at that verse in its context, the first description given of the good land is that it is a land "of flowing streams and pools of water, with fountains and springs that gush out in the valleys and hills." The Scriptures are overflowing with the metaphor of refreshing water for our souls.

In this section, let's shift our focus. We won't concentrate on the hard places. Not even on the refreshment we desire.

The most important word to our hope for restoration of our souls is the first word in our opening title: *He.*

That's where our hope goes when it needs refreshment—to the one who is the fountain of life.

WATER FOR PARCHED SOULS

Springs will gush forth in the wilderness,
and streams will water the wasteland.
– from ISAIAH 35:6 –

A summer downpour ended a hot and dry week, cooling the air and soaking the parched ground. Vegetables and flowers perked up. Even we perked up. Yes, we needed a rainy day.

Sometimes we live too long in a drought. We let busy schedules and the stuff of living crowd out our seeking of God, and we find ourselves parched and weary, exhausted and rapidly wilting. Sometimes we are scorched by searing pain or overwhelming trouble. Sometimes we're stumbling through a desert because of our own choice of the wrong path. Whatever the reason for the parched ground in our soul, the Father's promise is always the same to His children who cry out to Him:

> *"When the poor and needy search for water and there is none, and their tongues are parched from thirst, then I, the LORD, will answer them. I, the God of Israel, will never abandon them. I will open up rivers for them on the high plateaus. I will give them fountains of water in the valleys. I will fill the desert with pools of water. Rivers fed by springs will flow across the parched ground."* (Isaiah 41:17-18)

Can you feel the refreshing waters flowing through your soul?

Not just a few drops, but water everywhere. Rivers and fountains and springs and pools.

The book of Isaiah, especially, uses two metaphors of hope: the promise of water for parched souls, and the restoration and blossoming of the desert. We may be walking through a wilderness, or we may be looking in dismay at our lives and seeing nothing more than wasteland. But our hope knows that God brings reviving pools and streams to parched places and makes wastelands bloom again as lush gardens.

Does your soul need that reviving water?

Ask, Jesus said, and it will be given to you. Seek it, you'll find it.

Our Father promises He will answer.

In the parched and thirsty droughts of our lives, He never abandons us.

He can fill our desert with pools of water.

He hears and responds to that prayer we're using in this section: *I earnestly search for you. My soul thirsts for you in this parched and weary land.*

REVIVE ME!

I lie in the dust; revive me by your word.
– PSALM 119:25 –

Remember that verse above? We've already looked at it, back in the section on "Help for our hope."

I wanted to bring it back to mind again because when we are at the end of ourselves and our own strength, when we have nothing left in us, when we simply want to sink down into the dust and go no further, we do still have this hope.

We came from the dust of the ground. God's own breath gave us the life we have. Without that, we are still only dust, returning to dust.

If I do not always draw my breath from that Spirit of God living in me, I often sink back into the dust.

And I lie there, depleted. Exhausted.

What revives me then?

The second line of that prayer: His Word.

His Word also lives and breathes life as it waters my soul. It revives and brings me up out of the dust.

So this is just a short reminder of that earlier section: The Word of God helps our hope tremendously and revives us!

I like to mark those passages in my Bible that speak to my soul. Another option is to keep a journal, simply copying verses that give assurance and hope. In the parched times of my life, going back and reading His words to me, His loved child, always refreshes my soul.

Especially when I'm lying in the dust.

REFRESHMENT FOR PILGRIMS

*The LORD will guide you continually, giving you water
when you are dry and restoring your strength. You will be
like a well-watered garden, like an ever-flowing spring.*

— ISAIAH 58:11 —

Our pilgrimage takes us through all kinds
of terrain. In those parched stretches where we
grow thirsty and weary, we long for oases. Rest.
Refreshment. Sustaining water for our souls.

The Psalm prayer for this section is taken
from a longer verse:

*O God, you are my God; I earnestly search
for you. My soul thirsts for you; my
whole body longs for you in this parched
and weary land where there is no water.*
(Psalm 63:1)

This is the cry of a weary heart trudging
along in the desert. Have you been there? Are
you there now?

It reminded me of Psalm 84 that promises
this:

*What joy for those whose strength comes
from the LORD, who have set their minds
on a pilgrimage to Jerusalem. When they
walk through the Valley of Weeping, it
will become a place of refreshing springs.
The autumn rains will clothe it with*

blessings. They will continue to grow stronger, and each of them will appear before God in Jerusalem. (Psalm 84:5-7)

Do you see the focus once again? These refreshing springs come to pilgrims *who draw their strength from the Lord.* As we look constantly to the one who restores our souls, even valleys of weeping become a place showered with blessing.

We will all walk through these valleys or deserts; that will not be avoided. But as we depend on our Shepherd, He sends water for our souls along the way, supplying all we need in the weary desert.

REPENTANCE AND RESTORATION

Travel [in this] path, and you will find rest for your souls.
- from JEREMIAH 6:16 -

The more I read Scriptures, the more I see that God's commandments are not given to keep humanity under His iron fist. That's the lie that the enemy has whispered into our heads, just as he did to Adam and Eve.

God's instructions are meant, instead, to lead the way to a good life, a peaceful, secure, strong, and joyous life.

You might wonder why I use so many

Scriptures from the Old Testament. It's simply because they tell us so much about God, about us, and about our relationship with Him.

He does not change, He tells us in Malachi 3:6. And although everything in the external world has changed since Old Testament times, the story of human hearts either searching for or rejecting their Creator has remained the same throughout the centuries. So throughout that history in the Scriptures, we hear the Creator often guiding us along the right way back to Him.

> *This is what the* Lord *says: "Stop at the crossroads and look around. Ask for the old, godly way, and walk in it. Travel in its path, and you will find rest for your souls."* (Jeremiah 6:16)

First, let's remind ourselves of the meaning of that word *godly.* It does not mean *perfect.* Can anyone of us be perfect in our ways?

But it does mean seeking the way God says is perfect and good. It means desiring to live the way God intended for us to live when He created us in His image.

We come to many crossroads every day:

- A choice of whether to bless or curse the one who treats us badly.
- A choice of making a decision in favor of our own interests or the interest of others.

- A choice of lying or truth telling.
- A choice of offering up our sacrifices to the idols of the world or giving our living sacrifice to the Almighty God.

The list could go on and on.

When we reach those crossroads, STOP.

Look for the godly way, the good way, advises our Father. Traveling along that way, we will find rest for our souls.

There's one more line to this verse in Jeremiah 6. It's a short, sad line, and we all are familiar with the words: "But you reply, 'No, that's not the road we want!'"

We have all said those words. And we've also acted on them.

Let's jump to the New Testament, to Peter's powerful preaching after the Holy Spirit starts working in him. In the Temple, he tells the crowd,

"Now repent of your sins and turn to God, so that your sins may be wiped away. Then times of refreshment will come from the presence of the LORD." (Acts 3:19, 20)

The Father first tells us to choose the godly way at the crossroad if we want rest for our souls. But we sometimes fail to do that. We've said, "I want to choose my own way," and then we've often ended up in deadly quicksand, on muddy and rough paths, or in sun-scorched, parched deserts.

Then repentance is necessary, going back to the One who can restore our souls. And the wonderful thing is—He will do it!

Refreshment comes when we are again back in His presence.

⊱⊰ WEARY? FIND REST ⊱⊰

God has told his people, "Here is a place of rest; let the weary rest here. This is a place of quiet rest."
– ISAIAH 28:12 –

We hear the Creator Father constantly offering rest and refreshment to His people. "This is the way," He said. "I will give this to you." Yet humans constantly wandered away from that life-giving fountain.

Then God came to earth and lived as one of us and through Jesus Christ offered us everything our souls desire.

I've known the following verses forever. Now I want to re-learn them. I *need* to re-learn them.

Read this, if you can, as though you've never heard it before. I've always thought these verses hold such a depth of mystery and hope that we can hardly begin to comprehend it all. But I think we must begin.

Then Jesus said, "Come to me, all of you who are weary and carry heavy burdens, and I will give you rest. Take my yoke upon you. Let me teach you, because I am humble and gentle at heart, and you will find rest for your souls. For my yoke is easy to bear, and the burden I give you is light." (Matthew 11:28-30)

I've been asking the Spirit to teach me even more of what this means for my life. I'm still learning. But here are some of my thoughts thus far:

"Come to me." Jesus starts right off with saying He is the answer. He's the one to come to when we are exhausted from the weight of whatever heavy loads we carry. Guilt? Grief? Fear? Worry? Concern for others? Persecution? Restlessness? Discontent? Demands of life? Whatever it is, Jesus is the one to go to. Got that? *Whatever it is.*

We go to so many other places. To other people. To other ideas, especially the idols we have of self-sufficiency, pride, our own strength and powers, success (however the world defines it). And when we do go anywhere other than to Jesus, we are just chasing a mirage instead of going to the true fountain of living water.

There's a saying in the world today: "You've

got to know the right people." That can be applied here. Know the right Person to go to.

"and I will give you rest." I don't need to enlarge on that idea. Your soul tells you what that means.

"Let me teach you." These are the words that have been on my mind constantly. "Let me teach you," Jesus says to me. "Let me teach you about God. Let me teach you about living in the kingdom of heaven. Let me teach you about yourself and your mission on earth. Let me teach you about others and how God sees them and how you're to live with them. Let me teach you about those burdens you carry. Let me teach you."

"my yoke is easy to bear." And then there are these words about His yoke and the burden He gives. This is the most difficult part for me to understand. I grew up under a strong religious tradition that said I must do this and I must not do that and it was all a heavy burden. It is still a heavy burden because it can weigh me down, even though I've learned much about grace from experiencing His mercy in my own life. But is Jesus talking about His grace? Is he talking about His commandments? His commission of His mission to us? What is He saying? I'm still asking Him about this.

A friend shared that whenever she reads this verse, the thing she always sees is that Jesus carries the other half of the yoke. He's always carrying with us.

"You will find rest for your souls." Twice in these short lines, Jesus promises rest. Relief. Refreshment. That part I understand!

ᐳᐳᐟ LIFE-GIVING WATER ᐠᐸᐸ

For the Lamb on the throne will be their Shepherd. He will lead them to springs of life-giving water.
– **REVELATION 7:17** –

I can understand why the pillars of the religious establishment in Jesus' day were at their wits' end.

A good crowd had come to town for a religious festival, but now that fellow from Nazareth was standing out there shouting, "Is anyone thirsty? Then come to me, believe in me. Rivers of living water will flow out of your heart." Can you imagine the scene?

Just who did he think he was, anyway?

Well, they knew who *he* thought he was. And that was the thing that really upset them.

Once we stop chasing mirages and we find the true fountain of life, the real oasis in the desert, an amazing, miraculous thing happens. That Source comes to us and we become a part of Him.

Isn't that astounding?

And in the opening verse, we find that these streams of life-giving water will always be refreshing God's people. The Shepherd will be leading them to these springs, even in heaven!

I can't explain that or understand what it means, since it refers to a heavenly life that we only have glimpses of—but it is, nevertheless, a great hope to me.

And there's something else amazing about this water. It doesn't stop with our own refreshment.

These rivers of living water that God promises to refresh and revive His children—these are not for our sake alone; they're also so that we become conduits of that water.

Jesus said He was the light of the world; then He turned around and told those who followed Him that they were the light of the world. He said He was the living water; then He said that once we come to Him and drink, the living water will overflow, gushing out of us.

Why flowing *out* of our hearts?

Why not just "bubbling up" or "filling up"?

No, He said "flowing *out.*"

Could it be that our refreshment is also meant to flow out to others? To provide encouragement to flagging spirits? To walk alongside those who need help in the parched deserts?

When Jesus was talking about streams of living water, He was talking about the Spirit of God living within us. His presence in us is the true fountain of life. The real oasis in the desert. Living right with us, to slake our thirst in parched land, to revive us when we are ready to collapse from exhaustion.

He lives right here with us. Our own oasis of refreshment is never far away. Only a prayer away: "Revive me, Lord."

And then, the living waters become not only restorative for our own souls but also pour forth to refresh fellow pilgrims trudging wearily through their own deserts.

Amazing! We become part of our Father's plan for refreshing His weary children.

For more promises when you are parched and weary,
see the appendix for a list of additional Scriptures.

PRAYER FOR WISDOM:

Teach me your ways, O LORD, that I may live according to your truth!

– **from PSALM 86:11** –

THE GREAT TREASURE

ASKING OUT OF OUR NEED

For wisdom is far more valuable than rubies. Nothing you desire can compare with it.

- PROVERBS 8:11 -

Brick walls are good for us.

So is the end of our rope.

At wit's end? That's a fine place to be.

The end of the road or out of options? Also desirable situations

Yet I never hear anyone say, "Oh, good. I'm

finally up against a brick wall."

Where am I going with this? Right up on one of my favorite soapboxes—to rant about the cherished idol of our Western culture: our self-sufficiency.

The Supreme Court of our country—as I typed that title, I was struck with the irony, and so I was compelled to rephrase it: The court who is considered the highest in this country handed down a landmark decision just a few days before I wrote this. Not all the justices agreed with the decision. One of the dissenters believed the court had overstepped its authority and wrote, "Who do we think we are?"

A good question for all of us.

We think we are supreme. We think we are smart and strong and sufficient. We think we are educated and advanced. We've got what it takes, folks.

I'm no longer talking about the Supreme Court. I'm talking about you and me, small, ordinary people-on-the-street.

We've been conditioned to take pride in ourselves, in our intellect, and in all the other resources we so carefully try to build.

And it's not until we smash our noses into a brick wall or find ourselves hanging on to the last few threads of the rope that we finally realize the truth: We are destitute, and the idol we have created of *self* cannot help us.

As we meditate on the promise that God supplies everything we need for living our lives according to His ways, we must realize and admit our poverty and destitution. If we do not acknowledge our lack—of power, of health, of guidance, of love, of wisdom—we will never ask for all He can supply. As long as we're operating out of our own storehouse of resources, we'll never be awed by the Father flinging open the doors to His great treasure rooms. And that is why all hope starts with acknowledgment of our need.

For this hope of wisdom, in particular, Scriptures say:

> *If you need wisdom, ask our generous God, and he will give it to you. He will not rebuke you for asking. But when you ask him, be sure that your faith is in God alone. Do not waver, for a person with divided loyalty is as unsettled as a wave of the sea that is blown and tossed by the wind.* (James 1:5, 6)

Do we need wisdom to walk through this world?

Yes, if we want to walk Jesus' way.

Will God give us the wisdom we need?

Yes. Absolutely. It's promised. And He will be generous!

This is our hope that is certain, child of God: God will teach us His truth and ways, if we ask Him. He won't scold or lecture us, but will generously give us the wisdom we need. We bring our need, our emptiness, our nothing, to our Father and ask Him to fill it. I believe the Father is not only generous, He's also delighted to grant these requests.

But before we will even ask, we must admit that need. We must kick aside our pride in ourselves—tear down that idol—and put our faith in God alone. As long as we are still going to our idols to help us, God's wisdom cannot rule our lives.

The wisdom that God can give, Scriptures say, is the treasure above all treasures. Nothing else we chase after can compare to having this wisdom.

If I ask *What treasure do you desire most in this life?,* what answer springs first to your thoughts?

I confess, my first answer would not have been wisdom. I must even search my heart honestly and ask: Do I believe this? If I believe the Word of God is truth, then am I seeking wisdom more than anything else in this life?

I know that I have been conditioned and blinded by our idols of self-sufficiency and pride... So as preparation for these meditations, I'm asking the Spirit to show me what I lack and to teach me the humility to ask for this treasure from the Father.

⤳⤳ EVEN MORE UNDERSTANDING ⤳⤳

Give me understanding and I will obey your instructions; I will put them into practice with all my heart.

‒ PSALM 119:34 ‒

From Genesis to Revelation, this fact keeps popping up: God's view of things is quite different than ours.

Even Jesus, as a human being like us, was tempted to look at things from a human point of view instead of God's point of view. Matthew 16:21-23 gives that interesting account, when Jesus acknowledged that seeing things from a human point of view was a dangerous trap for Him.

It's clear in Scripture that there is something the world calls wisdom, and then there is true wisdom, that wisdom given by our Father, the wisdom that lines up with His truth.

Scripture is also emphatic that the "wisdom" of the world amounts to nothing; in fact, it will only lead us astray and keep us blind to the truth and wisdom of God. It's a dangerous trap for us, too.

How do we avoid that? It seems our culture is constantly pressing in on us, shaping our thinking, focusing our sights, and limiting our vision to an earthly level.

Let's rephrase that. We must go beyond labeling those influences as simply *culture.* That makes the danger seem much too benign. Let's understand this: it is the enemy at work, trying to destroy us and God's plan for us.

How do we escape the enemy's tricks and twisted perspective? How do we learn to see things from God's point of view? How can we see, as clearly as Jesus did, the traps laid for us?

We'll have to make a choice. The world's point-of-view? Or God's? When Satan tempted Jesus with this choice, he was aiming at Jesus' humanity. Satan uses the same strategies on us; we have the same decision to make.

Listen to Jesus' words to His disciples:

> *"To those who listen to my teaching, more understanding will be given, and they will have an abundance of knowledge. But for*

those who are not listening, even what little understanding they have will be taken away from them." (Matthew 13:12)

There it is again—we'll need to make a choice. We must choose if we want to know God's truth and wisdom and reality, or if we want to follow the world's. Do we listen to God's words, coming to us through Jesus, or do we ignore them or even deem them "not for us"?

I've always been overwhelmed with the depth of Colossians 2:3 which says that in Christ we'll find all the treasures of wisdom and knowledge. It's one of those verses that I try to grasp, but I feel as though it's so big and so deep and so impossible for my mind to understand that it's like trying to understand eternity. That verse is a difficult one for me. But it's there in Scripture, and it tells us that Jesus holds everything we need, even if we don't understand it fully.

1 Corinthians 1:30 seems equally difficult for me. There, Paul writes that *for our benefit* God made Jesus to be wisdom itself. The one thing I do grasp from these two verses is this: Jesus holds the key.

In contrast, the verse quoted from Matthew 13 speaks clearly: *Listen to Jesus' teaching.* And I think that listening here means more than just letting the words fall on your ears. It includes *doing.* Those who are following Jesus, who are taking His words into their heads and hearts, who are living out His words in their actions and speech, who are living (as we've been saying) in God's reality—these people will gain even more understanding.

That's what I want. *Even more understanding.*

You know the story of the wise man and the foolish man, building their houses on rock and sand. When telling that little parable, Jesus prefaced it by saying, "Anyone who listens to my teaching and follows it is wise, like a person who builds a house on a solid rock" (Matthew 7:24).

Could He be any clearer? These verses are much easier for me to understand. Jesus is truth. When we believe that, when we look to Him for truth, when we listen to His teaching and follow it—we will also grow in our wisdom and understanding.

ᔆᔆ᠁ THE CHOICE ᔆᔆ᠁

Your laws are always right.
Help me to understand them so I may live.
– **PSALM 119:144** –

Jesus said that following His teaching is wise and results in gaining even more understanding.

But...

Listening to Jesus, we soon realize that His teaching is often in direct opposition to what the world says is smart, wise, realistic, or practical.

And as we listen to Jesus and put His words into practice and find that the world thinks we're foolish, the enemy steps in and whispers his lies.

Satan would have us believe that we have the ability to judge whether or not the Creator's instructions to us are sound.

Stop a moment and think about how ludicrous that suggestion is.

Now, if you don't believe in the Creator Father, then you might as well stop reading here.

But if you do believe, think about this:

If we toss out God's instructions—His wisdom for the best way to live our lives—then we are tossing out reverence and awe of the one who created us, saying that *we know better.*

And that reverence and awe, or "fear of God", says Solomon, is the foundation and beginning of true wisdom.

God will let us go our own way. He will let us build our own little castles of grand ideas and self-importance. But Scripture is filled with warnings. We'll end up "eating bitter fruit" and choking on our own schemes (Proverbs 1:31). We'll spend our lives groping in the dark, always weary and hungry, looking everywhere, but always finding trouble and anguish and despair (Isaiah 8:20-22). Jealousy and selfishness motivate us then, and those give rise to all kinds of evil (see James 3).

Those warnings are not God's threats of punishment to keep us in line; those warnings simply state the consequences of following our own imperfect and poisoned ideas of "wisdom." You can look around and see those results everywhere in our world.

I can look at my own life and heart and see the results of following what *I thought* was best—in opposition to what God says.

But if we choose to pursue God's wisdom for living? That way has different results:

> *The instructions of the LORD are perfect, reviving the soul. The decrees of the LORD are trustworthy making wise the simple. The commandments of the LORD are right, bringing joy to the heart. The commands of the LORD are clear, giving insight for living.* (Psalm 19:7-8)

You'll make your own choice as to whose wisdom you will build on. But for my life, I want joy and insight for living. I want revival and refreshment for my soul. I want wisdom from the One who created me and knows me better than anyone. I want *to be able to live.*

God doesn't wave a magic wand and shower us with wisdom. Wisdom is built on the foundation of knowing and honoring the Creator. Then, as we follow His instructions, His wisdom grows in us.

ꙮ WHAT IS WISDOM? ꙮ

The wisdom from above is...
- from JAMES 3:17 -

Here we are, thinking about gaining wisdom— but what exactly is *wisdom?*

Scripture makes it clear that there is a false wisdom, touted by the world. Then there is true wisdom, with God as its source, embodied in Jesus, and available to God's children.

James, who wrote so much about how our faith and hope show up in daily living, gave us vivid pictures of how these two "wisdoms" act. (There are some pretty strong words here.)

If you are wise and understand God's ways, prove it by living an honorable life, doing good works with the humility that comes from wisdom.

But if you are bitterly jealous and there is selfish ambition in your heart, don't cover up the truth with boasting and lying. For jealousy and selfishness are not God's kind of wisdom. Such things are earthly, unspiritual, and demonic. For wherever there is jealousy and selfish ambition, there you will find disorder and evil of every kind.

But the wisdom from above is first of all pure. It is also peace loving, gentle at all times, and willing to yield to others. It is full of mercy and good deeds. It shows no favoritism and is always sincere.
(James 3:13-17)

His description of the pure wisdom from above sounds a lot like the *agape* love in 1 Corinthians 13, doesn't it?

And as I reflect on both this description of wisdom and Paul's description of love, I see how far from the mark I am. Those descriptions of the attributes of wisdom are not *me*.

That is, that's not the *me* that God first adopted and took under His wing and gave His name to.

But, as His child now, I am learning His ways. Did you see that clue in the first sentence from James? *If you are wise and understand God's ways...*

How about this as a definition of wisdom: The ability to see things as God sees things, to think His thoughts, and to act and speak accordingly.

Is that presumptuous? Is it too bold to hope that we can understand God's ways when He has said that His thoughts and ways are so far above ours?

I don't think so. Not if God keeps His promises.

And my hope is convinced that He does.

So how can we understand God's ways and thoughts?

We have an astonishing promise that answers that question. Read on...

KNOWING GOD'S MIND

For his Spirit searches out everything and shows us God's deep secrets.
– from 1 CORINTHIANS 2:10 –

Does that title sound too presumptuous? Maybe even sacrilegious? It *is* bold, isn't it?

Yet we have a promise that is equally bold. Stunning, to my mind. Read the verse above, if you haven't already.

We are shown and can know God's deep secrets.

Aren't you amazed by that statement?

I am.

We've looked at this verse before, but it's so amazing to me... let's look again.

If the pure wisdom from above is being able to see things as God sees them, to think His thoughts, and to act and speak accordingly, how is such wisdom going to come to my mind, heart, and will—all of which are bent on my own selfish motivations and interests?

Through transformation—what I think of as a second *creation.*

You remember how God "breathed the breath of life" into the sculptured dust, and Adam became a living soul. When we come to Jesus and become sons and daughters of God, He breathes His own Spirit into us... and a new creation comes alive. The transformation begins as the Spirit He breathes into us begins to change us and create a new person.

It is the Spirit who gives us our connection to God's thoughts.

> *For his [God's] Spirit searches out everything and shows us God's deep secrets. No one can know a person's thoughts except that person's own spirit, and no one can know God's thoughts except God's own Spirit.* (from 1 Corinthians 2:10, 11)

"I know exactly what you're thinking." You probably have heard that, or said it yourself. Two people may know each other so well that they've learned how the other's mind works.

But we have a connection with God that is even more intimate. Just as those first breaths from God gave man life, so the breathing of His Spirit into each of His children gives them a connection to Him—a connection to His thoughts, His secrets even!

The word *secrets* here means *something that was previously hidden.*

Doesn't this amaze you?

The kindness of God that brought us to this place is amazing.

The connection He creates with us through His Spirit is amazing.

His plan for our transformation is amazing.

This is part of the Spirit's work—to help us understand the mind of God. The Spirit teaches us, reminds us, and mold us. One of His important tools is the Word of God. While He is teaching us, He even gives us the power to act and speak according to His wisdom.

God is aiming at a complete transformation of me—and of you, son or daughter of the Almighty Father.

Here's what Paul wrote to new Christians:

Don't copy the behavior and customs of this world, but let God transform you into a new person by changing the way you think. (Romans 12:2)

That's the only way pure wisdom from above is going to permeate my mind and my will—by the Spirit of Christ connecting me to the Father's thoughts and transforming the way I think.

The second part of that verse is the hope we children of God can be certain of:

Then you will learn to know God's will for you, which is good and pleasing and perfect. (Romans 12:2)

Then we begin to see and understand how God sees things. Then we start perceiving God's reality. Then we begin to grow in the pure wisdom given from the heavenly Father.

Amazing. Amazing. Amazing.

And although it sounds so bold to make this claim—my hope is depending on this connection to God's thoughts as I yearn to walk wisely in this world.

ᵕᵕᵕᵕ WISDOM: KNOWING GOD BETTER ᵕᵕᵕᵕ

All the while, you will grow as you learn
to know God better and better.

- from **COLOSSIANS 1:10** -

Perhaps this question should have been asked at the beginning, rather than at the ending of this section: What's the point of desiring wisdom?

Does that seem like an inane question? (Yes, just one letter away from *insane*.)

Of course, we want to live wisely, to make good decisions and choices that honor our calling as God's children and Christ's representatives on earth. Those are all good reasons to seek wisdom.

But there is an even greater longing in us that sends out a cry to our Creator Father, asking for wisdom.

It is the longing to know Him better, to understand His "deep secrets," and to see ourselves and this world as He sees everything.

This is part of the Spirit's work in us. The world will never know the Creator through human "wisdom." Only the Spirit living in us gives us the connection that pulls us ever closer into His thoughts and into knowing Him deeply.

May our prayer for ourselves and each other be this:

We ask God to give you complete

knowledge of his will and to give you spiritual wisdom and understanding. Then the way you live will always honor and please the LORD, and your lives will produce every kind of good fruit. All the while, you will grow as you learn to know God better and better. (Colossians 1:9-10)

Children of God, let's desire the pure wisdom from above.

Ask. Knock. Seek Christ.

And our God will give generously and abundantly as we get to know Him better and better.

For more on the promise of wisdom,
see the appendix for a list of additional Scriptures.

PRAYER FOR GUIDANCE:

Teach me how to live, O LORD,

Lead me along the right path.

– **from PSALM 27:11** –

WALKING THE BEST PATH

ᴥᴥ "I WILL GUIDE YOU" ᴥᴥ

I will guide you along the best pathway for your life. I will
advise you and watch over you.

- **PSALM 32:8** -

"If you're in downeast Maine this morning,"
said the pastor on a bright Sunday morning,
"there's no way you can miss the glory and
awesome work of God."

Those of us in the pews smiled and nodded.
A few said *Amen.* Everyone understood what he

meant. The day was spectacular, the kind of day when you have to be outside because you want to fill up with the beauty and you don't want to waste one minute of it.

The next day, Monday morning, I opened my eyes at 4:30 and watched as the entire sky flushed with countless shades of pinks and purples. The water, from one end of the bay to the other, reflected the rosy radiance. A glorious morning. Again, I was in awe of God's creation.

Then, getting to work, I turned to one of the Scriptures I was studying for this section, and I was utterly amazed. This is what struck me:

> The LORD directs the steps of the godly.
> He delights in every detail of their lives.
> Though they stumble, they will never fall,
> for the LORD holds them by the hand.

That's from Psalm 37:23-24.

Many years ago, when I was stumbling along, someone pointed out these two verses to me. They encouraged me at a time when I thought I was a hopeless mess. First, there is that promise that even though I sometimes stumble, my Father is still holding me. Second, I can go to Him with any little detail of my life. Nothing is too trivial to take to my Father.

But when I read the verses on that magnificent Monday morning in Maine, it was a different time in my life; and that day, it was the first line that filled me with amazement and gratitude: The God who created all of that glory of land, sky, and sea directs my steps! *My* steps! Every little detail of my ordinary, "average" life, the Almighty Creator cares about.

Amazing. Yet—this is what God says is reality!

His Word to me is that He will guide me along the best pathway for my life, be my advisor, and watch over me. The One who created this universe has promised me that. Why should I fear going forward, when that bridge of hope is before me?

AVAILABLE: WONDERFUL COUNSELOR

He made their hearts,
so he understands everything they do.
– PSALM 33:15 –

One of the pitfalls of working out of my home is that my computer is only steps away from the kitchen. Snacks are too accessible. And willpower is too unreliable.

But I've learned something that's been helpful in controlling my snacking. Often when we go to the cupboard looking for something to munch, we are not hungry but, in fact, we are thirsty. We mistake our thirst for hunger, and so when we munch on potato chips, we end up cheating our bodies of the water we need and also doing harm with the snacks we consume.

Once I understood that, I found it much easier to control unnecessary snacking. (Key word: unnecessary!) Instead of a cookie, I'd drink a glass of water. And it satisfied me. Benefits, all around.

Just as we sometimes stand in front of the refrigerator or cupboard and look for something (even though we don't know quite what), when we need guidance and direction, we often go looking for... what? Do we properly identify our thirst? Or are we scrounging around in all the wrong places to satisfy what is actually our need for a Wonderful Counselor?

Oh, for a Wonderful Counselor! How many times in your life, even in the last week, have you wished for a wonderful counselor?

Someone who understands you to the core.

Someone who can step outside the circles you've been running through in your head, or step outside the conflicts raging in your relationship, or step outside the mess you've gotten yourself into, and can show you the truth of your situation.

Someone whose advice you can trust to be

wise and right on target.

Someone who loves you.

Where do you find that person?

One of the first promises in prophecy about the baby to be born to bring light and hope to the world was that He would be a Wonderful Counselor.

> *For a child is born to us, a son is given to us. The government will rest on his shoulders. And he will be called: Wonderful Counselor, Mighty God, Everlasting Father, Prince of Peace.* (Isaiah 9:6)

Let the weight of those words sink into your bones. The Messiah who came to this world is the Wonderful Counselor. Just what we need.

And then let each of these names fill your mind, because this is who your counselor is:

MIGHTY GOD,

EVERLASTING FATHER,

PRINCE OF PEACE.

Again, amazing! (This section may be filled with too many exclamation points. Living on the promise that God will guide us in the best paths is living with marvelous expectation and deserves many exclamation points.)

Amazing, that I can go to the Mighty, Eternal

God and Prince of Peace for advice and counsel.

Amazing, that He has promised to guide my steps. My ordinary, daily, insignificant-only-me steps.

Why would I even choose to snack? Instead, I am thirsty—for a Wonderful Counselor, the one who understands everything about me.

⸢⸴⸴⟋ BUILDING ON BEDROCK ⟍⸲⸲⸣

The LORD is my shepherd. He guides me along right paths, bringing honor to his name.
— from **PSALM 23:1, 3** —

"The road moves." *What?* Had I heard my friend correctly?

We were standing on the rocks at water's edge outside a small cottage, looking across the bay to the horizon where these waters meet the Atlantic Ocean. To picture this place, think of a finger of land stretching out into the sea. At the tip, the cottage sits on only an acre of land. The "finger" leading to this place is the narrow causeway we had driven across to reach the cottage.

"The causeway. It moves from year to year."

I was about to make a remark that where I come from, roads stay put. But the thought occurred to me that they actually don't. Pavement is laid down, but it sinks and cracks and heaves up, and, yes, moves about just like this causeway that shifts under the stresses of wind, waves, and weather.

It reminded me of Jesus' words:

"Anyone who listens to my teaching and follows it is wise, like a person who builds a house on solid rock. Though the rain comes in torrents and the floodwaters rise and the winds beat against that house, it won't collapse because it is built on bedrock.

"But anyone who hears my teaching and doesn't obey it is foolish, like a person who builds a house on sand. When the rains and floods come and the winds beat against that house, it will collapse with a mighty crash." (Matthew 7:24-27)

Jesus, the Wonderful Counselor, assures us that His teaching is the bedrock on which we can build our way in life. If we are wise, we take heed to His words and let them guide us in our living. Our hope can be confident that He leads along a road that will not shift or sink or collapse.

‹‹‹‹‹ THE GUIDANCE WITHIN ›››››

And I will ask the Father, and he will give you another
Advocate, who will never leave you. He is the Holy Spirit,
who leads into all truth. The world cannot receive him
because it isn't looking for him and doesn't recognize him.
But you know him...

– from JOHN 14:15,16,17 –

I cannot explain the *how* of this hope. I know that it seems preposterous to those who do not believe in a living God who is in the lives of His children.

But the children of God who live by faith hold a hope that frees us from paralysis and moves us forward. Our hope knows that the Spirit of God lives in us and guides our steps.

Jesus said the Holy Spirit would always be with us, guiding, teaching, and leading us into truth (John 14:16-17, 26).

As Jesus moved from town to town speaking about His Kingdom and performing miracles, I'm sure some of the disciples missed some of the things He said. I mean, they couldn't be with the man every minute of every day, could they? He often went off by Himself, or sometimes He sent disciples on errands or off on bigger missions. They surely had to take care of some family responsibilities at times. So I'm sure, hungry as they might have been for what He was saying and doing, they missed out on some of His teaching.

But today, Jesus guides and teaches each one of His disciples personally and individually. You and me. He is with us always, every minute, every step, in every situation. Because He is "in us."

Now how do we explain that? Just exactly where is He in us?

I don't know.

But I believe it.

It's one of those hopes we are certain of, a hope that our faith acts upon because we know it's true: God, living in us—mysteriously, super-naturally, miraculously, in the all-encompassing spiritual realm—guides us and teaches us.

In His guiding and teaching, He produces a certain kind of life, a life that goes beyond our human nature, tendencies, and capabilities. It's impossible to cover all that in a few short pages, but you can read all about it in Galatians 5:16-26.

Look again at the words from Jesus promising the Holy Spirit (the opening verses from the Gospel of John). The Spirit will always be with us, always guiding.

However, the world won't receive, recognize, or even look for the Spirit. Of course not.

But we do, children of God. We do. Because our hope depends on Him and His guidance.

It's the reason God gave us the gift of His Spirit in us—to guide us on our journey.

✦✦ GUIDED IN THE DARK ✦✦

When I am overwhelmed, you alone know
the way I should turn.
– from PSALM 142:3 –

Almost ten years ago, I made what many people might call a rash decision. I left a good job to begin freelancing. I had no projects lined up, no business plan, and, really, very little idea how I was going to develop an income.

All I knew for certain was that this was a step God would bless. And He did. Many things happened that I considered miracles, quite unexpected, improbable events that slowly forged my new life. This life I now have is God's doing, and it is wonderful!

Psalm 32:8 was my beacon as I navigated through the first years. I depended on God's promise that He would guide me to the best paths, He would advise me and watch over me. I was certain of it. I put my life on the line because of that promise. And yes, I often reminded God that I was depending on Him to keep that promise.

It was one of the times in my life that I knew with great clarity that God was leading down a new path.

But there have been many other times when His guidance has not been that clear. Times that

I've stewed for weeks about a decision. Times that I've begged for guidance, but never seemed to get an answer.

What about those times?

"I wish God would leave me a note on the countertop." That's a line my sisters and I have often uttered in conversations. Aren't there times when you would like to have handwriting on the wall or a voice from heaven to direct you?

We wish, sometimes, for everything to be clear, distinct, unambiguous, and safe.

What about those nights when we're still wide awake at 3 a.m., or those days when our thoughts race around in circles asking *how? where? when? should I? and God, why don't you show me exactly what to do?*

Hebrews 11 says that faith hopes in what it does not see. Faith steps out in the darkness, not knowing what waits, but feeling the hand that guides and the love that surrounds.

"How can I know God has asked me to follow a certain path?"

"Can I be certain that I haven't just talked myself into believing this?"

"How do I know where God is leading me?"

Those are questions most of us have asked at one time or another. They seem to be complicated, deep questions.

But perhaps the answer is this simple: God says He will guide us. That, He says, is reality we can depend on.

In Isaiah 42, God promises to lead His people Israel. If we read the entire chapter, we discover that Israel had wandered away from God; they were "blind" and living in darkness. Yet God says He will guide His blind people down a new and unfamiliar path, smoothing their way, lighting their darkness.

In Psalm 139, David sings about the amazing hope that no matter where I walk, God's hand will guide me. Even when I walk in the dark.

And then Jesus repeated the promise: He will always be with us. The Spirit, the Comforter, the Helper, the Guide, will never leave us. He is living with us to help us and to guide our thinking and behavior—even when we're confused, or see no answer in a tangled situation, or are too exhausted to see two steps in front of us. The apostle Paul wrote that the Spirit helps us pray when we don't know what to pray. My hope knows that He also helps us *move,* even when we don't know how or in which direction to move.

These examples all show God's ongoing guidance of His people. Even though we are less than perfect. Even when we're overwhelmed and feel as if we're walking in the dark.

God's hand is always on my life. And His promise is that He will always guide me, whether or not I can *feel* or *see* it.

This doesn't mean we charge through life, willy-nilly, shrug our shoulders, and say, "Oh, God will guide us through." It does mean that we turn our hearts and minds over to Him and ask that, even in our puzzlement and confusion and short-sightedness, He will move us along in the right direction.

I am still depending on the promise in Psalm 32:8. You can too, fellow pilgrim. Even when we're walking in the dark, our hope can depend on what God says is reality.

DISCIPLINE GUIDANCE

"For the LORD disciplines those He loves."

– from HEBREWS 12:6 –

"Oh, Lord, no! Please, not today. Please, help! Help!"

My whole body tensed, ready for the gripping pain.

Do you ever get those leg cramps when a muscle in your calf is caught in a spasm so powerful that you can barely breathe and all you can do is grit your teeth and tough it out for a minute or so?

Then the grip releases, and you relax—but a lingering ache remains in that muscle for as long as a week, and you limp about.

That's what I felt coming on that morning, and, well, I just didn't want to endure the cramp or the after-effects. I had too much planned for the next few days to be hampered by a sore leg. (Muscle cramps are never conveniently scheduled.)

So I called for help. Yes, I prayed about a leg cramp.

The tightening immediately stopped, and the muscle relaxed.

That has never happened before. I've never been able to do anything to stop a cramp from coming on. This time, it had to be my Father's direct intervention.

"Oh, thank you, thank you, thank you!" I said.

And then came the word from the Spirit.

This is exactly what you should be doing with those thoughts you've been having... call for My help the minute they start. The minute they start!

You see, my thoughts had been going down the wrong road for a few days—down paths laid out wide and smooth by my natural, selfish tendencies. And although I know that poison grows along that path, I let my thoughts go that way. I let them go. As a result, I'd been unhappy and discontented, and the poison had seeped first into me and then from me into one of my close friendships.

I got the message that morning, with the lesson of the leg cramp.

When my thinking starts wandering off on the wrong path, I need to call for help from the Spirit at once. Otherwise, that poison of wrong thinking renders me powerless and leaves me with pain that lasts for days if not weeks or months. So I need to call for His help immediately.

Sure enough, that very day, my mind started going off in the wrong direction yet again. So I did call for help.

And help came!

And the usual ache left in my muscle after a leg cramp?

That never came.

I know my simple incident of the leg cramp is just a small thing compared to the discipline that God sometimes puts us through to keep us on the right path. Many of us have had to go through some hard, painful times in order for God to teach us necessary things. But whether the incident is small or if it's life-shattering, the point is this:

The LORD is good and does what is right;

*he shows the proper path to those who go
astray. He leads the humble in doing right,
teaching them his way.* (Psalm 25:8-9)

I could tell you of other times when I was
horribly off-track, but I'd rather focus on the
good news that God acts to get us back on the
proper path.

He doesn't write us off as incorrigible and
hopeless. He doesn't say, *That's it. I'm done with
her. She'll never learn. I've had enough of her
foolishness and stubbornness.* He still guides us,
bringing us back to the right way after we've gone
wandering—or bolting—off on our own reckless
and destructive ways.

In Psalm 73, the songwriter tells of a time
that he was bitter and envious and resentful.
(God should have sent him an early-morning leg
cramp.) But still, he belonged to God, and God
guided him back to a proper perspective. Like a
loving parent or mentor, the Father will correct
and train and guide us when we are so out of line.

Jeremiah, too, knew he needed God's guiding
correction. One of his prayers can be ours:

*I know, LORD, that our lives are not our
own. We are not able to plan our own
course. So correct me, LORD, but please be
gentle.* (Jeremiah 10:23)

All of us would probably add that last line in our prayers, too!

Of course correcting discipline is painful. Of course we'd rather not have to learn the hard way. But we often persist in our waywardness and make this type of guidance necessary.

The opening verse from Hebrews 12 is preceded by a verse that says, *Don't give up when God corrects you.* Later in the same chapter, we're given both the promise and the hope:

> *God's discipline is always good for us, so that we might share in his holiness... afterward there will be a peaceful harvest of right living for those who are trained in this way.* (Hebrews 12:10-11)

That's what I desire—a peaceful harvest of right living.

So if I need my Father's discipline to keep me on the right path, then so be it. I want His guidance. I want that harvest.

﹅ﺯﺀﻷ SHEPHERDED FOREVER ﻷﺀﺯ﹅

I give them eternal life, and they will never perish. No one
can snatch them away from me.
– The Great Shepherd, JOHN 10:28 –

We began this book with the question,
desperate for many: *How do I get through today?*

We've seen that God shepherds His people,
providing what we need, caring about every
detail of our daily lives, showing us the right
paths, and correcting our course when necessary.

But the story is even bigger than all of that.
God supplies what we need today—and He has
much more in mind.

After the Israelites escaped from the Egyptians
through the Red Sea, Moses led the people in a
song of praise to the Almighty for providing a
way out of the danger. The song included these
lines:

> *"With your unfailing love you lead the*
> *people you have redeemed. In your might,*
> *you guide them to your sacred home."*
> (Exodus 15:13)

God has an ultimate purpose in His leading.
He has far more in sight for us than the next
few hours. If we can catch a glimpse of His
perspective, it will change how we approach
those next few hours, too. And our Psalm prayer

asking Him to show us the right paths will take on a far deeper meaning.

Those words from Exodus are also for God's people in every era of history: God rescues people because He loves them, and He guides them back to Himself.

Our stories are quite like the story of the ancient Israelites. Let's get the big picture—

God created people to be like Him and enjoy a relationship with Him. Yet we have been "traitors and rebels from birth" (from Isaiah 48:8), and we (like the Israelites) find that ignoring God's guidance lands us in captivity to other powers.

> *This is what the* Lord *says—your Redeemer, the Holy One of Israel:*
>
> *"I am the* Lord *your God, who teaches you what is good for you and leads you along the paths you should follow. Oh, that you had listened to my commands!*
>
> *Then you would have had peace flowing like a gentle river and righteousness rolling over you like waves in the sea."* (Isaiah 48:17-18)

At the time Isaiah received those words from God, the people of Israel had decided they were done with God and they wanted to choose their own way. So they did, and disaster followed.

Instead of the gentle river of peace and right living they might have had, they saw their country and temple destroyed, and their conquerors shipped them off to live in Babylon under the rule of a pagan king.

Yet God still promised them rescue. A Great Shepherd would come to gather His flock and provide all they needed. Eventually, the Shepherd would lay down His own life so that His sheep could live.

That's our story. And whenever one hears the Shepherd's voice and follows Him, God the Father plants His own Spirit within that person, to guide and lead to life. The apostle Paul wrote that "Letting the Spirit control your mind leads to life and peace" (Romans 8:6). That's a promise for disciples of all time and for us, as we face today and all it will bring.

But here's the rest of the story: Following the Shepherd leads to life, not only for the duration of our walk here on earth, but on into a life that does not end. Yes, immortality.

In Revelation, the book that gives us glimpses into that future, we read that "the Lamb will be their Shepherd" (Revelation 7:17).

I cannot pinpoint the time or place of this verse. As a matter of fact, it refers to a time when there is no time or place. It is a glimpse we're given into eternity.

And even then, our Shepherd will be leading us!

May I tell you how that changes things for me?

I remember a time in my life when thinking about eternity brought anxiety. Not because I was afraid of hell. That question had been settled between God and me. But I was anxious because eternity is all unknown. How do we even begin to comprehend it? What is heaven? What will that life be like?

Have you had similar apprehensions?

Now, as I think about that future, my hope is simply in the care of my Shepherd, who will let no one snatch me away from Him, as He guides me today, in many different ways, supplying all that I need, guiding always to life-giving water, going on forever, whatever and wherever that may be, guiding me to His sacred home.

For more promises of guidance,
see the appendix for a list of additional Scriptures.

PRAYER WHEN DISCOURAGEMENT THREATENS:

I will be glad and rejoice in your unfailing love, for you have seen my troubles, and you care about the anguish of my soul.

– **PSALM 31:7** –

DEFENSE AGAINST DISCOURAGEMENT

༺⚘ WE'RE NEVER ALONE ⚘༻

The LORD is close to the brokenhearted; he rescues those whose spirits are crushed.

- **PSALM 34:18** -

As we come to the close of our conversations, let's do a bit of review. Some of this section will be repetition, reminders of things we've already meditated upon. I think we do well to bring back to mind, especially, some of God's words that will help us when discouragement reaches out its ugly claws and tries to grab us.

Let's look at the help and hope that God supplies when we're discouraged. What bridges of hope has He given us that can keep us moving forward, even in our "low" times? Maybe you're in the clutches of discouragement right now. If so, I pray as I write that Jesus the Rescuer opens your eyes to see Him fighting for you.

Where do we go when we are discouraged? When we need to have our energy revived and our faith bolstered, what do we do?

We might seek out friends—and godly friends are a gift from the Father to give us support and encouragement. But we all have times when even our dearest friends do not understand the weariness of our heart. Or even if they do understand, they have no antidote for the heavy burden of discouragement. Discouragement makes us feel alone.

Hear Jesus' words: "All who love me will do what I say. My Father will love them, and we will come and make our home with each of them" (John 14:23).

Isn't this good news? Hope knows and clings to this: We are not alone! The God of all comfort and the God who has promised to supply all we need lives with us.

☙ EVEN IN MY DISCOURAGEMENT ☙

*My heart was bitter, and I was all torn up inside. I was so
foolish and ignorant... Yet I still belong to you; you hold
my right hand. You guide me with your counsel, leading me
to a glorious destiny.*

— from **PSALM 73:21-24** —

The storm blew in with high winds and waves
of hard rain. Trees toppled, power lines sagged,
and debris blew across lawns and gardens. The
next morning, rows of corn lay flat, beaten to the
ground by the pounding elements. They looked
tattered and exhausted.

As I drove down the valley, the sight of
those corn stalks brought tears to my eyes. Not
for sympathy for the corn, but because I was
feeling exactly like that—battered and flattened
by a storm. Would the young stalks survive and
somehow bounce back up and produce their crop?
Could they survive after such a beating? How
would my hope bounce back? *Would* it, *could* it
survive and flourish again?

The prophet Isaiah repeats to God's people
the Lord's reassurance for times of uncertainty,
promises of strength for days of weariness, and the
hope of courage for moments of fear. Reassurance,
strength, and courage—all things that drain away
when we are in the pit of discouragement.

Your heavenly Father says,

"For I have chosen you and will not throw you away. Don't be afraid, for I am with you. Don't be discouraged, for I am your God. I will strengthen you and help you. I will hold you up with my victorious right hand.

"For I hold you by your right hand — I, the LORD *your God. And I say to you, 'Don't be afraid. I am here to help you...'"*
(Isaiah 41:9-10, 13)

Don't be discouraged. I am your God, and I am here to help you.

Your Father has chosen you and will be with you through everything!

Isn't that amazing?

And so, my hope does not lose heart, no matter what obstacles tower ahead, because the Lord of the universe is here, with me.

In the storm, He is my refuge.

When I know I am too weak, when I fear I am losing the battle, when I see no way to turn, He will keep me going.

When I think I struggle alone, His powerful hand of victory is working for me.

When I am tattered and torn and exhausted, He is there with healing and refreshment.

He says, "I am always with you. I am here to help."

He is holding me, even in my discouragement.

↜↝ STANDING UNDER POURED ↝↜ OUT LOVE

But each day the LORD pours his unfailing love upon me.

- **PSALM 42:8** -

"But I trust in your unfailing love. I will rejoice because you have rescued me. I will sing to the LORD because he is good to me" (Psalm 13:5-6).

This declaration of trust in God sounds like it was written by a committed, devoted, on-fire, unshakeable Christian, right? You know—one of those people who seem to have everything together, everything's going great, and their lives are shining models of what we all think we should be.

Read it again, and notice that first word: *But.*

These words came, instead, from a soul in a dark valley. The preceding lines of the psalm called out a desperate plea that might echo in our own hearts.

The writer was in a painful time of anguish and struggle. He saw no light at all in the darkness. Everything seemed to be going against him, and he even began to wonder if maybe God was not paying attention. He felt so separated from God that he asked, "Have you forgotten me? Where are you?"

His struggle sounds familiar, doesn't it? We're

battered by hard times, times of doubt, times of loneliness, times of discouragement. We drag through dark, dark valleys, and we wonder if all of God's promises are true. Can I believe Him? Will He really do what He says? Can I depend on Him?

But... no matter what we might feel, God says His unfailing love surrounds His children. He cares about the anguish of our souls. He holds us in His hands, and He will not hand us over to the enemy. He will help us and put our feet on solid ground.

Psalm 147:11 says that God delights in "those who put their hope in his unfailing love."

Even when it feels as though we are lost and alone in the dark valley, if we can say, "I will trust in Your unfailing love. I know You care about my anguish," then we will also come through to the place where we can say, "I'll sing to the Lord, because He is good to me."

Psalm 42 follows the same pattern. Again, we hear deep discouragement. The writer's heart is breaking. Raging seas and surging tides sweep over him. He is wandering around, bent under a black burden of grief.

But again the writer comes back to what the Lord has promised: "But each day the LORD pours his unfailing love upon me" (Psalm 42:8).

See yourself, discouraged child of God, standing under His poured out love!

Even in the loneliness and the dark and the pain, hope stands on the bridge of promise, under that outpouring, and says, "I will trust in your love, Lord!"

❧ "DIDN'T I TELL YOU?" ❧

God is able, through his mighty power at work within us,
to accomplish infinitely more than we might think or ask.
‑ from **EPHESIANS 3:20** ‑

How would you feel? Imagine that your dear sister (or spouse or parent) was sick, and you were certain that one of your friends could help her. You send a message to him, *Come quickly.*

But you get no response to the message. The friend does not come. And your dear one dies.

What would you think? *Doesn't he care? How could he ignore us when we desperately needed him?*

I'd be plenty discouraged. I'd be awash in grief at my loss and disappointment in my friend. I'd probably be feeling betrayed and pretty low.

That's what happened to Martha. Her brother Lazarus was sick, and Jesus didn't show up to save him.

"I wish you would have been here. You could have saved him," said Martha when Jesus finally did visit the grieving family.

"Martha, no one who believes in me will ever die. Do you believe me, Martha?" asked Jesus.

"You know I do. I've believed in You from the very beginning," affirmed Martha.

Yet when they walked to the cave where Lazarus had been entombed and Jesus ordered them to roll away the stone at the entrance, Martha objected.

"He's been dead for four days. The smell will be terrible."

We are just like Martha! We say we believe all the promises of God. We believe in His power. We believe He works for our good. We believe He watches over us and cares for us and protects us. We believe in His goodness and His love. We believe. Yes, we believe.

But when we're faced with what we call "hard facts of life" and discouragement sets in, we talk and act as though the Lord of the universe just can't handle the smelly stuff. Like Martha, who blurted out the truth of her unbelief, what we say both to ourselves and others shows our own lack of faith.

Jesus loved Martha. His response to her was, "Didn't I tell you that you would see God's glory if you believe?" (John 11:40)

I don't think Jesus was scolding Martha. I think He was reminding her, gently, "Martha, there is so much more... if you'll just believe in me, you'll see what God can do."

He loves us, too. He reminds us, gently, as we falter in discouragement or tremble in fear of defeat, "If you believe, you will see God's glory. Believe in me, trust me. I have things for you beyond your imagination, beyond anything you think is possible."

Yes, those are the promises for those who believe.

My hope hangs onto promises like that.

AFTER THE PIT, A NEW SONG

Let all who are helpless take heart.
Come, let us tell of the LORD's greatness.
- from PSALM 34:2-3 -

Many of the Psalms speak for all of us whose hearts are set on pilgrimage. Like us, David and other writers trusted in God and believed in God's unfailing love and faithfulness. Like us also, he sometimes landed in the mud at the bottom of the pit of despair.

And so, I keep going back to the Psalms.

Sometimes we feel ourselves sinking into the

mire of discouragement, the muck of... what?
Fatigue? Worry? Low self-esteem? Loneliness?
Guilt? Temptations? Fill in that last word yourself.
What is it that drags you down, discourages you,
and keeps you from walking on solid ground and
singing new songs?

David wrote:

> I waited patiently for the LORD to help
> me, and he turned to me and heard my
> cry. He lifted me out of the pit of despair,
> out of the mud and the mire. He set my
> feet on solid ground and steadied me as
> I walked along. He has given me a new
> song to sing, a hymn of praise to our God.
> Many will see what he has done and be
> amazed. They will put their trust in the
> LORD. (Psalm 40:1-3)

Although David wrote this in the past tense,
not all of the muck and mud is behind him. If you
read the entire chapter 40, you'll see him crying
for help yet again. *Rescue me! I've lost courage! I
can't find my way out!*

It's as though David began writing to
remember what God has done in the past, and to
remind himself that God can, and will, pull him
out of the pit he's now in.

We see it again and again in David's writings.
At times, he even thinks God has forgotten him.

Yet he reminds himself that God's love surrounds him and God has been good to him.

Here's a lesson for me. God has pulled me out of the mud so many times when I could not free myself, when I could see no escape, when all I could do was cry, "Help! I'm sinking!" I'm guessing He has rescued you from the muck, too. He always hears our cries. His love for us is never forgetful or absent.

And then, He also sets our feet on solid ground, steadies us as we go onward, and gifts us with a new song of praise. Out of our times in the pit come new strengths and new thankfulness. We will sing new songs!

We will. Our hope knows that.

And look at the last line. When we're in the depths of the pit, it's hard to see any possibility of good in tomorrow. But as in everything else, God will even use this hard time to bring people to Himself.

You can even use my time in the pit, Lord?

These three verses remind us to remember— remember what our Lord has done in our lives. Sitting in the mud at the bottom of the pit, we must remember.

Cry for help and rescue, yes. But do not lose heart, because hope knows that He hears and He rescues—and strengthens and renews our song.

ANTIDOTES FOR DISCOURAGEMENT

Now all glory to God, who is able to make you strong,
just as my Good News says.
— from **ROMANS 16:25** —

There's a short little verse in Romans that holds important advice for us when discouragement claws at us. Three antidotes for discouragement:

Rejoice in our confident hope.
Be patient in trouble,
and keep on praying. (Romans 12:12)

#1 *Rejoice in our confident hope.* Read and believe His promises. That's what we've been doing in these pages—celebrating the hope we have been given, learning to live "with great expectation" because we trust God. Even in the pit, remember how good the Lord has been to you and rejoice in your hope.

Hold tightly to that hope, because we know God can be trusted to keep His promises!

#2 *Be patient in trouble.* Oh, this is so difficult for me. I think I must "fix" things... or God must fix things. Why must we have hard times? Why must we suffer for no apparent reason? Why do some people carry such heavy burdens of trouble, like Job? God has the power to change everything with one word—why does He let this trouble and that trouble go on? Why does He not save me from this?

Yet our hope knows that God is in control and He has a purpose for us and for everything He does. He works for our good in every circumstance and His timing is always perfect. He is with us in the midst of every trouble. If He doesn't calm the storm, we can ask Him to calm us.

Be patient, O my soul.

#3 *Keep on praying.* Our relationship to Jesus is the lifeline by which we live and breathe and bear fruit. "Never stop praying," Paul wrote in his first letter to the persecuted Thessalonica Christians (1 Thessalonians 5:17).

Prayer is the antidote to worry and the way to peace (See Philippians 4:6).

Observing this third guideline will make the first two possible—prayer helps us to be patient in trouble and keeps our focus on the God of all hope.

Rejoice in your hope, child of God.

Be patient through all trouble.

Keep on praying.

༷ WITH SUCH A PROMISE, HOW ༷ CAN WE GIVE UP?

Let us hold tightly without wavering to the hope we affirm,
for God can be trusted to keep his promise.

‒ **HEBREWS 10:23** ‒

While I was a college student, I had a summer job that was funded by a grant. My assigned tasks did fill a need, but I didn't have enough work to keep me busy for the required hours. On many days, I had to search for something more to do, odd jobs and trivial tasks, until the clock released me to leave the office.

Later in life, I held a job that was often overwhelming simply because there was too much to do in each day. I worked long hours, many times gulping down lunch at my desk.

I much prefer the second kind of job, even though it was more stressful. At the second job, I knew that everything I did counted for something.

Let this promise today inject you with just a few more ounces of energy:

> *So, my dear brothers and sisters, be strong and immovable. Always work enthusiastically for the Lord, for you know that nothing you do for the Lord is ever useless.* (1 Corinthians 15:58)

You may not be feeling "strong and

immovable" right now, but how can we give up if we have a promise like this?

Doesn't it make a difference to know that everything—*everything*—we do for the Lord is important? We are not just putting in our time, going through the motions of discipleship. Everything we do for Him matters in His Kingdom!

One of Satan's most effective strategies to derail our discipleship is to convince us that what we are doing has no or very little importance. Or perhaps he whispers other lies to you: "You're not qualified to do this; someone else could do this better" and "This is making no difference. What you do has had no effect. All your effort has meant nothing. Might as well give it up" and "You're not making any progress at all. Are you sure this is the right road?"

My dear brothers and sisters in God's family, stand strong and immovable against the lies! If the Spirit is producing fruit in your life, if He moves you to do *anything,* no matter how small it might seem (remember the cup of cold water), do not give up, because nothing you do for the Lord is useless.

The hope held in this verse grows even fuller when we look at its context. In 1 Corinthians 15, Paul has just written long paragraphs about the promise of the resurrection of our bodies and the certainty that we will live forever. He ends it by saying, "So don't give up. Stand strong. Whatever we do for the Lord is very important."

Apparently, the effects of what we do here on earth will not be limited to this hour, this day, or the length of our earthly lives. What we do for the Lord has effects that reach into eternity.

This is a good place, as we close this book, to offer my thanks to those who have encouraged me through the many years of work that went into the *Hope Knows* books, and thanks also to those of you who have prayed for this project. Whatever you have done for the Lord is very important!

This hope is our encouragement to be strong and to stand immovable. There will always be the low valleys of discouragement, and sometimes we even fall into the pit of despair for a time. But we have dependable bridges that keep us moving forward.

Paul writes in another letter that we can be sure we will reap a harvest of blessing if we don't give up. (Galatians 6:9)

Even when we're tired and discouraged, nothing we do for our Lord is ever useless. This promise picks us up again and again, to stand, strong and immovable, and holding tightly to our hope.

For more encouragement,
see the appendix for a list of additional Scriptures.

APPENDIX

ADDITIONAL SCRIPTURES FOR STUDY AND ENCOURAGEMENT

We travel many roads in life, and there is not a one that God has ignored or forgotten or did not know about when He planned the bridges of promise to help us along the way.

Then He generously gave us His Word, letting us know what He will do for His people, so that we will be encouraged and confident in our journey.

If you want more comfort and assurance of each section's specific hope, here are more Scriptures. The lists are not complete; you'll find hope on every page of Scripture if you ask God to show it to you. But here's a starting point.

THE GIFT OF HOPE:

Psalm 9:10; Psalm 31:15, 21-22; Psalm 33:4; Psalm 39:6-7; Psalm 42:5, 11; Psalm 43:5; Psalm 56:4; Psalm 62:5-6; Psalm 78:7; Psalm 119:49-50; Psalm 146:5-6; Proverbs 10:24-25; Isaiah 51:3; Isaiah 55:3; Jeremiah 17:5-8; Lamentations 3:24; Micah 7:7; Romans 4:16-21; Romans 5:1-5; Romans 12:12; Romans 15:4, 13; Colossians 1:11-12; Hebrews 6:18-20; Hebrews 10:23-25; Hebrews 10:35, 36; Hebrews 11:27; 1 Peter 1:3, 6; Revelation 1:17-18.

EVERYTHING WE NEED:

Psalm 23; Psalm 34:8-10; Psalm 37:23; Psalm 39:6-7; Psalm 55:22; Isaiah 9:6; Isaiah 28:16; Isaiah 41:13; Jeremiah 17:7-8; Matthew 6:25-33; John 14:1; John 15:4-5; Romans 8:31,32; 1 Corinthians 1:7-9; 1 Corinthians 12:4-7; Galatians 2:20; Ephesians 1:19-20; Ephesians 3:20; Ephesians 4:11-16; Ephesians 5:8-9; Philippians 4:19; Colossians 1:9-10; Colossians 1:27; Colossians 3:1-3; 1 Timothy 4:8; Hebrews 13:20-21; 1 Peter 1:3, 6; 1 Peter 4:10-11; 1 Peter 5:7; 2 Peter 1:3-4; 1 John 4:13-16.

PROMISES FOR THOSE WHO WAIT:

Psalm 25; Psalm 27:13-14; Psalm 31:7, 14-15, 24; Psalm 33:18-22; Psalm 37:7, 34; Psalm 40; Psalm 62:1, 5-8; Psalm 119:81-88; Proverbs 20:22; Isaiah 30:18; Isaiah 40:26-31; Isaiah 41:10, 13; Isaiah 64:1-4; Lamentations 3:25-26; Micah 7:7; John 14:1; Romans 8:28 and 12:12; Philippians 1:6; Colossians 1:11-12; 2 Thessalonians 3:3; Hebrews 10:23, 36; James 1:12; James 5:11; 1 Peter 1:6; Revelation 3:11.

HELP FOR OUR HOPE:

Deuteronomy 29:29; Psalm 19:7-9; Psalm 94:19; Psalm 111:7-8; Psalm 119 (Make your own list of all the things the Word does for us); Isaiah 40:8; Jeremiah 15:16; Matthew 5:18; Matthew 24:35; Luke 21:33; Romans 15:4; Ephesians 6:17; 1 Thessalonians 2:13; Hebrews 4:12; James 1:21; James 1:25; 2 Peter 1:4.

CARRIED IN HIS ARMS:

Psalm 23; Psalm 33:18-22; Psalm 36:5-10; Psalm 55:22; Psalm 66:9; Psalm 68:19; Psalm 91; Psalm 103; Psalm 106:24; Psalm 121; Isaiah 41:17-20; Isaiah 46:3-4; Matthew 6:24-34; Luke 12:7, 22-34; Romans 8:31; Philippians 4:6, 7, 19; Hebrews 13:5; 1 Peter 2:25; 1 Peter 5:7; 2 Peter 1:3; 1 John 3:1; Jude 1:24; Revelation 7:15-17.

"I'M HERE TO HELP YOU":

Exodus 15:1-18; Deuteronomy 9:3; Deuteronomy 31:6; Psalm 10:17; Psalm 18; Psalm 28:7-8a; Psalm 34; Psalm 37:5; Psalm 40; Psalm 46:1; Psalm 63:7-8; Psalm 69:32-33a; Psalm 91:14-15; Psalm 103:1-5; Psalm 107; Psalm 115:9-11; Psalm 116:1-9; Psalm 118:6-9; Psalm 121; Psalm 124; Psalm 145:14-20; Psalm 146:3-6; Isaiah 30:18-19; Isaiah 41:8-10, 13; Isaiah 43:1-4, 7, 10, 12; Nahum 1:7; John 14:15-17, 26; John 16:33; Romans 8:26a, 28; Philippians 2:13; Philippians 4:13; Hebrews 2:18; Hebrews 4:14-16; Hebrews 13:5-6; Hebrews 13:20-21. (And so many more.)

FINDING NEW STRENGTH:

1 Chronicles 16:11; 2 Chronicles 16:9; Psalm 18; Psalm 22:19; Psalm 23:3; Psalm 28:7-8a; Psalm 29:11; Psalm 68:35; Psalm 73:26; Psalm 84:5-7, 12; Psalm 89:15-17; Psalm 105:4; Psalm 138:3; Psalm 139:9-10; Psalm 146:3-6; Isaiah 40:28-31; Isaiah 41:10; Haggai 2:4; John 15:5; 1 Corinthians 1:8-9; 1 Corinthians 16:13; 2 Corinthians 1:21-22; 2 Corinthians 4:7; 2 Corinthians 12:8-10; Ephesians 3:16-20; Ephesians 6:10; Philippians 4:13,19; Colossians 1:11-12 and 2:6-7; 1 Thessalonians 3:12-13; 2 Thessalonians 1:11-12; 2 Thessalonians 2:16-17; 2 Thessalonians 3:3, 5; 2 Timothy 4:17; 1 Peter 4:10-11; 1 Peter 5:10.

WINNING THE BATTLE:

1 Chronicles 5:20; Psalm 9:9-10; Psalm 18; Psalm 20:1-5; Psalm 23:5; Psalm 25:14-16, 20; Psalm 28:7-8a; Psalm 31:1-5; Psalm 34:6-7; Psalm 54:7; Psalm 56:9; Psalm 59:9-11; Psalm 62:1-2, 5-8; Psalm 91:2-3, 9-10; Psalm 141:8-9; Psalm 143:9; Proverbs 18:10; Isaiah 40:29, 31a; Isaiah 41:11-16; John 16:33; Romans 6:6-7, 10-11; Romans 8:2, 26, 35, 37; 1 Corinthians 1:7-9; 1 Corinthians 10:12-13; 1 Corinthians 15:57-58; Galatians 5:16-17; Ephesians 6:10-18; Philippians 4:6-7, 13; 2 Thessalonians 3:3, 5; Titus 2:14; Hebrews 2:16-18; Hebrews 4:15-16; James 1:2-5, 12; James 4:7; 1 Peter 1:6-7; 1 Peter 4:12-13; 1 Peter 5:8-10; 2 Peter 1:3-4; 2 Peter 2:9; 1 John 4:4-5; 1 John 5:3-5.

RESCUE FROM AN EMPTY LIFE:

Psalm 16:11; Psalm 22:26; Psalm 23; Psalm 34:8-10; Psalm 36:7-9; Psalm 40:4-5; Psalm 70:4; Psalm 84:5-7, 10-12; Psalm 116:7-9; Psalm 118:8; Isaiah 55:1-3, 12-13; Jeremiah 17:7-8; Matthew 7:7-11; Luke 12:29-32; John 10:10; John 15:11; John 17:13; Romans 8:31-32; Romans 15:13; 2 Corinthians 9:8; Philippians 4:19; James 1:17; 1 Peter 1:18.   (Many more in the text.)

GOOD THINGS OUT OF HARD PLACES:

Deuteronomy 8:2-15; Psalm 23:4-5; Psalm 31:1-9; Psalm 46:1-11; Psalm 84:5-7; Psalm 94:12; Psalm 105:16-19; Psalm 119:67-72; Psalm 126:5-6; Isaiah 27:7-9; Isaiah 48:8-11; Isaiah 61:3; Daniel 11:35; Daniel 12:10; Matthew 5:4, 10-12; Luke 6:22-23; Luke 21:12-15; John 14:16; John 15:18-21; John 16:33; John 17:13-20; Acts 5:40-42; Roman 5:3-5; Romans 8:15-17, 28-39; Romans 12:12; 1 Corinthians 1:7-9; 2 Corinthians 1:3-5; 2 Corinthians 4:6-10, 15-18; 2 Corinthians 6:10; 2 Corinthians 8:1-2; 2 Corinthians 12:8-10; Colossians 1:11-14; 1 Thessalonians 1:6-7; 2 Thessalonians 3:3, 5; 2 Timothy 3:10-13; 2 Timothy 4:5; Hebrews 2:18; Hebrews 4:14-16; Hebrews 5:7-8; Hebrews 10:32-38; Hebrews 12:5-13; James 1:2-4, 12; 1 Peter 1:6-7, 9; 1 Peter 2:18-21; 1 Peter 4:12-16, 19; 1 Peter 5:10, 12.

REFRESHMENT FOR THE WEARY:

Psalm 19:7; Psalm 23:2,3a; Psalm 34:18; Psalm 36:9; Psalm 63:1; Psalm 84:5-7; Psalm 103:3-5; Psalm 107:4-9; Psalm 119:49-50; Psalm 119:81-82; Psalm 143; Isaiah 12:3-5; Isaiah 35:3-7; Isaiah 41:17-20; Isaiah 44:2-3; Isaiah 49:10-13; Isaiah 55:1-3; Isaiah 58:11; Jeremiah 6:16; Jeremiah 17:7-8; Matthew 11:28-30; John 4:10-14; John 7:37-39; Acts 3:19-20; Revelation 7:15-17; Revelation 21:5-7.

THE GREAT TREASURE:

Psalm 19:7-8; Psalm 86:11; Psalm 111:10; Psalm 119:98-104; Psalm 119:130; Proverbs 1:1-33; Proverbs 2; Proverbs 8:11; Proverbs 9:10; Proverbs 15:33; Proverbs 16:16; Proverbs 17:24; Isaiah 8:11-22; Isaiah 48:17-18; Matthew 7:24-27; Matthew 13:11-12; Luke 6:46-49; John 14:16,17, 26; John 15:26; John 16:12-15; Romans 12:2; 1 Corinthians 1:21; 1 Corinthians 2; Ephesians 1:16-17; Colossians 3:16; 2 Timothy 1:14; James 1:5-8; James 3:17; 1 John 2:26, 27; 1 John 5:20.

WALKING THE BEST PATH:

Exodus 15:13; Psalm 5:8; Psalm 23; Psalm 25:4-10; Psalm 27:11; Psalm 32:8; Psalm 37:23-24; Psalm 73:23-24; Psalm 119:105, 133; Psalm 139:9-10, 23-24; Psalm 143:8,10; Proverbs 3:5-6, 11-12; Isaiah 30:18-22; Isaiah 42:16-17; Isaiah 48:17-18; Isaiah 58:11; Jeremiah 10:23-24; John 10:1-16; John 14:16-17, 25-26; John 16:13; Galatians 5:16-25; 2 Thessalonians 3:5; Hebrews 12:5-12; Revelation 3:19; Revelation 7:17.

DEFENSE AGAINST DISCOURAGEMENT:

Psalm 13; Psalm 23:6; Psalm 27:13-14; Psalm 31; Psalm 33:4; Psalm 34:18; Psalm 37:7, 34; Psalm 40:1-5; Psalm 42:5-8; Psalm 73:21-24; Psalm 77:1-15; Psalm 90:14-17; Psalm 119:49, 50, 81-82; Psalm 121; Psalm 147:11; Proverbs 3:5-8; Isaiah 41:9, 10, 13; Isaiah 46:4; Lamentations 3:19-26; Luke 6:20-23; John 11:40; John 16:33; Romans 2:7; Romans 12:12; 1 Corinthians 1:8-9; 1 Corinthians 15:58; 2 Corinthians 4:15-18; 2 Corinthians 7:5-6; Galatians 6:7-10; Philippians 1:6; Philippians 4:6-7; Colossians 1:11-12; 1 Thessalonians 5:23-24; 2 Thessalonians 2:16-17; 2 Timothy 2:12; Hebrews 3:14; Hebrews 10:23, 32-36; Hebrews 12:10b-13; Hebrews 13:21; James 1:12; 1 Peter 1:3-9; 1 Peter 4:19; 1 Peter 5:7-11; Jude 24; Revelation 2:7; Revelation 3:11-12; Revelation 14:12-13.